启航 高职英语综合教程

主　编　李经宁　刘家华

副主编　谢　颖　钱　婧

编　者　谈　积　潘　妍
　　　　苏　攀

清华大学出版社

北　京

内 容 简 介

本教材旨在培养学生的英语应用能力，让学生能够在日常交际场合用英语进行有效交流，学以致用。本教材共有12个单元，主题涉及介绍、天气、学习、健康、饮食、运动、节日、金钱、旅行、娱乐、购物、就业等，均为学生熟悉的话题，浅显易懂。本教材内容编排由易到难，循序渐进，涵盖听、读、写、说四个板块，并在单元最后安排了一个项目活动，作为整个单元能力的综合和提升；语言选择上以简单实用为主，不追求长句难句，便于学生理解、内化、应用。

本教材适合高等职业院校公共英语课程使用，也可作为职场人士提高日常英语交际能力的参考用书。

图书在版编目（CIP）数据

启航高职英语综合教程 / 李经宁，刘家华主编. —北京：清华大学出版社，2021.7（2023.8重印）
ISBN 978-7-302-58497-1

Ⅰ.①启… Ⅱ.①李… ②刘… Ⅲ.①英语—高等职业教育—教材 Ⅳ.①H319.39

中国版本图书馆CIP数据核字（2021）第121302号

责任编辑：刘　艳
封面设计：子　一
责任校对：王凤芝
责任印制：丛怀宇

出版发行：清华大学出版社
网　　　址：http:// www. tup. com. cn，http:// www. wqbook. com
地　　　址：北京清华大学学研大厦A座　　邮　　编：100084
社 总 机：010-83470000　　邮　　购：010-62786544
投稿与读者服务：010-62776969，c-service@tup.tsinghua.edu.cn
质量反馈：010-62772015，zhiliang@tup.tsinghua.edu.cn
印 装 者：大厂回族自治县彩虹印刷有限公司
经　　销：全国新华书店
开　　本：210mm×285mm　　印　　张：10.25　　字　　数：220千字
版　　次：2021 年 8 月第 1 版　　印　　次：2023 年 8 月第 3 次印刷
定　　价：58.00元

产品编号：092665-02

前 言

近两年来国家陆续发布关于职业教育的重要文件。2019 年 1 月 24 日，国务院印发《国家职业教育改革实施方案》（以下简称《方案》）。《方案》指出，"要以习近平新时代中国特色社会主义思想为指导，把职业教育摆在教育改革创新和经济社会发展中更加突出位置。" 2021 年 4 月 1 日，教育部颁布《高等职业教育专科英语课程标准（2021 年版）》，对高等职业教育专科阶段的英语学科核心素养作了明确界定，即职场涉外沟通、多元文化交流、语言思维提升和自主学习完善。2021 年 4 月 12 日至 13 日，全国职业教育大会在京召开，习近平总书记对职业教育工作作出重要指示："职业教育将更加注重培养实践能力。技能培养必须在实践中学习、磨炼，这是客观规律。实践证明，越接近真实的工作环境、越接近生产一线、越接近实际操作过程，职业教育培养的人才质量就越高。"

高职英语作为一门公共基础课程，如何能够提升学生的综合素养，接近职业教育对真实工作环境、生产一线的要求，一直是令广大教师感到困惑的问题。

为了解决高职英语课程的痛点，即学生普遍对英语不感兴趣，觉得学不会英语，更用不上英语，2018 年 6 月，扬州工业职业技术学院大学英语课程组开始了英语教学改革之路。课程组教师一直在探索，2019 年明确的基于项目式教学的英语教学改革也在实践中砥砺前行，将英语课堂生活化、实用化、情境化，力求学生在英语表达时做到敢、能、准，基于项目，在实践中让学生更加深刻地掌握英语语言技能。

由于没有一套合适的基于项目式教学的教材，课程组教师经历了学习研究、收集资料和编写试用的阶段。本教材的出版，凝聚了扬州工业职业技术学院英语教师的辛勤努力。教材每个单元紧扣日常生活，通过教材学习，学生可以提升英语实际应用能力，尤其是听说能力。另外，本教材对中国传统文化也有一定篇幅的介绍。

课程以 12 个项目作为主线，项目主题遵循由校内到校外、由单一到多元的原则，囊括了学生日常生活中最常见的主题：介绍、天气、学习、健康、饮食、运动、节日、金钱、旅行、娱乐、购物、就业等，在此基础上，经过整理、编辑构成本教材的 12 个单元。每个单元包含 6 个部分，即热身（Warm-up）、听力（Listening）、阅读（Reading）、写作（Writing）、口语（Speaking）、项目（Project）。热身部分用于导入单元主题；听力和阅读部分均为信息输入，其中阅读部分有两篇文章，Text 1 用于精读，Text 2 用于泛读；写作和口语部分作为信息输出，口语表达对于高职学生而言较为困难，安排在单元主要内容之后，让学生有足够多的信息输入后，再开口讲英语；项目部分作为整个单元能力的综合和提升。内容编排上，先输入，再产出，最后以完成项目作为总结。教材的总体难度不大，便于学生自主学习能力的培养，适合高等职业院校公共英语课程使用。本教材生词选取主要基于《高等职业教育专科英语课程标准（2021 年版）》词汇表，不带任何标记的词汇为学生入学时应掌握的词汇，带 * 标记的词汇为基础模块词汇，带 ** 标记的词汇为拓展模块词汇或超纲词汇，每个单元的词汇表和最后的词汇总表都有标记。

本教材编写分工如下：刘家华负责编写第一单元、第四单元；谢颖负责编写第六单元、第十二单元；钱婧负责编写第二单元、第十一单元；谈积负责编写第七单元、第八单元；潘妍负责编写第九单元、第十单元；苏攀负责编写第三单元、第五单元；李经宁负责审订全部内容。教材阅读部分的素材主要摘自报纸、杂志、网络文章并进行适当修改。

由于编者水平有限，经验不足，本教材的不当之处，敬请专家、同行和读者批评指正。

主编

2021 年 5 月

Contents

Unit ⑥ Sports 63

Unit ⑦ Festival 75

Unit ⑧ Money 87

UNIT **1**

Introduction

Warm-up

Choose the right option to complete the following dialogue.

> A. Nice to meet you, too.
>
> B. Have you ever been there?
>
> C. Haven't seen you for ages!
>
> D. Paul, let me introduce my friend Mr. King to you.
>
> E. How's everything?

Paul: Hi, Smith. (1)_____

Smith: Hi, Paul. (2)_____

Paul: Pretty good! And you?

Smith: Fine, thank you. (3)_____

Paul: Nice to meet you, Mr. King.

King: (4)_____

Smith: Where are you from?

King: I'm from Suzhou. (5)_____

Smith: Yes, it's a beautiful city.

Paul: Are you used to living here?

King: No, not yet.

Paul: Don't worry. Everything will be fine.

Part One Listening

A Listen to the recording and choose the proper response.

1. A. No, you can't.   B. Yes, I am.
   C. Please don't.   D. Fine, thanks.

2. A. He is leaving by bus.   B. He has a big family.
   C. He is living in a small town.   D. He is a lawyer.

3. A. She's tall with dark hair.   B. She's an English student.

C. She's interested in music.   D. She's a friend of mine.

4. A. Hurry up.   B. Nothing left.

C. Me, too.   D. No more.

5. A. Yes, I have.   B. I like the city.

C. It's a famous city.   D. Yes, it is.

B **Listen to the dialogues and choose the best answer to each question.**

1. A. She's a worker.   B. She's a nurse.

C. She's a car driver.   D. She's an engineer.

2. A. Tim left France last week.

B. Tim won't leave Paris until next Wednesday.

C. Tim has gone to China.

D. Tim will leave for China next Monday.

3. A. He didn't like the weather in the north.

B. He didn't like the places.

C. He didn't like the food.

D. He didn't like it at all.

4. A. She is on business.   B. She is attending a meeting.

C. She is on holiday.   D. She is on a lecture tour.

5. A. She has not heard of Prof. Savio.

B. She is a good friend of Prof. Savio.

C. She has not heard of Prof. Savio's brother-in-law.

D. She does not know Prof. Savio's brother-in-law.

C **Listen to the following dialogue and fill in the blanks with what you hear.**

Li Ming: Excuse me! Are you Peter Brown?

Peter Brown: Yes, I am. What's your (1)_____ please?

Li Ming: I'm Li Ming.

Peter Brown: Nice to meet you.

Li Ming: Nice to meet you, too.

Peter Brown:	I am from the U.K. Where are you from?
Li Ming:	I'm from Nanjing, China. I study Art in college. What's your (2)_____?
Peter Brown:	(3)_____. This is the first year of my college life. I'm still not used to the life here.
Li Ming:	I'm a (4)_____ too. Don't worry. You'll get used to the life here. Everyone on the (5)_____ is very (6)_____. If you (7)_____ any problem, don't hesitate to ask me for help.
Peter Brown:	Thanks, I will. By the way, where is the (8)_____? I like playing table tennis in my (9)_____.
Li Ming:	It's at the northwestern corner of the campus, near the dining hall.
Peter Brown:	I see. Oh, there goes the bell. I must (10)_____ now. See you later.
Li Ming:	See you.

Part Two Reading

Text 1

The Master of Investment: Warren Buffett

Born on August 30, 1930 and bred in Omaha, Nebraska, Warren Buffett has led an **extraordinary** life. Looking back of his childhood, one can see the budding of a savvy[1] businessman. Even as a young child, Buffett was pretty serious about making money. He used to go door-to-door and sell soda pop. He had also worked at his grandfather's **grocery** store. At the **ripe** age of 11, Buffett bought his first **stock**.

When his family moved to Washington, D.C., Buffett became a paperboy for *The Washington Post* and its rival[2], the *Times-Herald*. Buffett ran his five paper routes like an assembly line[3] and even added magazines to round out[4] his product offerings. While still in school, he was making $175 a month, a full-time wage for many young men. When he was 14, Buffett spent $1,200 on 40 acres[5] of farmland in Nebraska and soon began collecting rent from a tenant[6] farmer.

Already a successful small-time[7] businessman, Buffett wasn't **keen** on going to college but ended up at Wharton at the University of Pennsylvania—his father encouraged him to go. After two years at Wharton, Buffett **transferred** to his parents' alma mater[8], the University of Nebraska in Lincoln, for his final year of college. There Buffett took a job with the *Lincoln Journal* supervising[9] 50 paperboys in six **rural** countries.

Buffett **applied** to Harvard Business School but was turned down, which was one of the worst admissions[10] decisions in Harvard history. The **outcome** was that he attended Columbia Business School, where he studied under Benjamin Graham, the father of securities[11] **analysis** who provided the **foundation** for Buffett's **investment** strategy.

Buffett's investment strategy mirrors his lifestyle and overall **philosophy**. He is a creature of habit—same house, same office, same city, same soda—and dislikes change.

Buffett's view of inherited[12] money also departs from the norm. When his daughter needed $20 to park at the airport, he made her write him a check for it. As for charity, Buffett's strict **standards** have made it difficult for him to give much away. He has **established** the Buffett Foundation, designed to accumulate[13] money and give it away after his and his wife's deaths—though the foundation has donated millions to different organizations.

---

1. 机智的，聪慧的 2. 对手 3. 生产流水线 4. 完成 5. 公顷 6. 租户，佃户 7. 不太重要的；小规模的
8. 母校 9. 管理 10. 录取 11. 证券 12. 继承的 13. 积累

Vocabulary

extraordinary**	/ɪkˈstrɔːdnri/	*adj.*	非凡的；特别的
grocery	/ˈɡrəʊsəri/	*n.*	食品杂货店
ripe**	/raɪp/	*adj.*	成熟的
stock	/stɒk/	*n.*	股票；股份
keen*	/kiːn/	*adj.*	（对……）着迷的，渴望的；热心的
transfer	/trænsˈfɜː(r)/	*v.*	转学；调动；转移
rural*	/ˈrʊərəl/	*adj.*	乡村的，农村的
apply	/əˈplaɪ/	*v.*	申请，请求
outcome*	/ˈaʊtkʌm/	*n.*	结果；效果
analysis**	/əˈnæləsɪs/	*n.*	（对事物的）分析；分析结果
foundation**	/faʊnˈdeɪʃn/	*n.*	基础；基金会
investment*	/ɪnˈvestmənt/	*n.*	投资
philosophy**	/fəˈlɒsəfi/	*n.*	哲学

| standard | /ˈstændəd/ | n. | 标准，水平；规格，规范 |
| establish | /ɪˈstæblɪʃ/ | v. | 建立，创立，设立 |

Exercises

A Decide whether the following statements are true (T) or false (F) according to the passage.

(   ) 1. Warren Buffett didn't make any money until he was 11.

(   ) 2. While still in school, Buffett could earn more money than many full-time workers in the U.S.

(   ) 3. Buffett applied to Harvard University and was admitted.

(   ) 4. Buffett's daughter was financially dependent on him.

(   ) 5. The Buffett Foundation has accumulated a great amount of money.

B Fill in each blank with the proper form of the word given in the brackets.

1. You need to write a letter of _____ (apply) to apply for a job.

2. The job involves gathering and _____ (analysis) data.

3. A number of beaches in this country fail to meet European _____ (standard) on cleanliness.

4. Yangzhou Polytechnic Institute was _____ (establish) in 2004.

5. The task is _____ (extraordinary) difficult for a young man.

C Complete the following sentences in English according to the Chinese.

1. 这家电影制片厂正迁往好莱坞。
   The film studio is _____ to Hollywood.

2. 我们应该把知识应用于实践。
   We should _____ knowledge _____ practice.

3. 结果仍不确定。
   The _____ was still uncertain.

4. 我母亲一直有着很高的道德水准。

My mother has always had high moral _____.

5. 华为技术有限公司成立于 1987 年。

Huawei Technologies Co., Ltd. was _____ in 1987.

Text ②

Best Actress at the Golden Rooster Awards

Actress Zhou Dongyu, 28, has been in top form in recent years.

Zhou was nominated for Best Actress at the Golden Rooster Awards on Nov. 7, 2020 for the third time. She will become the first post-90s Chinese actress to receive the best actress award at three events, if she is honored with the award on Nov. 25 at the awards ceremony in Xiamen, Fujian. Previously, she took home the Best Actress at the Golden Horse Awards and the Hong Kong Film Awards for her performances in *Soul Mate* and *Better Days*, respectively.

Zhou debuted in the 2010 movie *Under the Hawthorn Tree* and rose to fame overnight at age 19. In the movie, she played an innocent schoolgirl called Jingqiu. At that time, she was criticized for her acting and appearance. Zhou is not a girl that fits the typical standards of beauty with big eyes. "It would be so much better if I had bigger eyes," she told *Southern People Weekly*.

But Zhou didn't let her appearance stop her. Instead, she tried to play different roles to break the stereotype that she could only play a schoolgirl. She came to prominence with her role in *Soul Mate*, in which she plays Li Ansheng, a girl with a rootless free spirit.

Later, she played a mentally disabled girl in *On the Balcony*. To portray her character, she watched a lot of documentaries. "That's one of the most challenging things about my job: to have to understand characters and scenarios I've never encountered before," Zhou told *Variety*.

Now, Zhou's acting has been recognized by the public and professionals in the showbiz industry. What's more, she has embraced the way she looks.

Women in the industry are now judged on their talent, ability and the freedom to be themselves instead of beauty standards and appearances, Zhou said at a Kering Women in Motion Talk. "[It] makes me happy...I believe audiences love seeing characters and real people that they can relate to."

Exercise

Answer the following questions according to the passage.

1. Where will the awards ceremony of the Golden Rooster be held?

_____

2. What awards has Zhou won?

_____

3. In which movie did Zhou first appear?

_____

4. When did Zhou become famous in China?

_____

5. Do the public and professionals recognize Zhou's acting?

_____

Part Three Writing

A Study the following sample of self-introduction.

Hello, I'm Wang Hua. You can call me Mr. Wang, or my English name Joey. I was born in 1982 in a small village in Xuzhou, Jiangsu and grew up there. I left my hometown for Nanjing Normal University in 2001. I've been working at this school since my graduation from The School of Foreign Languages and Cultures at the university in 2005. And I have more than 15 years' work experience.

I have a big family. I live with my parents, my wife and two children. My wife works in a middle school. We have two boys. The elder one goes to elementary school, and the younger one goes to kindergarten. I love them all very much.

In my spare time, I like reading books, watching movies and traveling.

I am your English teacher this semester. I hope we can get along with each other and be good friends for the rest of our lives.

Best wishes for you.

B Write a self-introduction with about 150 words, including your name, hometown, major, hobby, family, etc.

_____

_____

_____

_____

_____

_____

_____

_____

_____

_____

_____

C Complete the letter of introduction according to the Chinese letter.

扬州工业职业技术学院化学工程学院

2020 年 11 月 18 日

亲爱的王斌教授：

　　兹介绍持信者李平到您处，请您指导她的实验报告写作。她去年毕业于新华中学，一向是三好学生，品德高尚，学习勤奋，聪明伶俐。

　　李平的父亲供职于扬州化工厂，和我相交二十多年，情谊甚深。指导李平一事，请大力协助为盼。

　　致以衷心的谢意，并祝全家安好！

挚友

王福敬上

College of Chemical Engineering

(1)_____

November 18, 2020

Dear Professor Wang Bin,

It gives me much pleasure to introduce to you (2)_____, Li Ping, who is going to ask you to help her with her experiment report writing. She graduated from Xinhua Middle School last year. Always a three-good student, she is (3)_____.

Li's father, who works at Yangzhou Chemical Factory, has been (4)_____ for more than twenty years. Whatever you do for her will be really appreciated and considered a personal favor to me.

Please accept my heartfelt thanks and with kindest regards to you and yours!

(5)_____,

Wang Fu

Part Four 🗼 Speaking

A Read the following sentence patterns concerning introduction.

Starter	Response
Hello, I'm...What's your name?	Hi, My name is...
Good morning! Are you...?	Yes, I'm...
Where are you from? Where do you come from?	I am from... I come from...
What's your hobby?	I like traveling/fishing/swimming...
What's your major? What are you majoring in?	My major is... I'm majoring in...

| How do you think of yourself? | I'm friendly/hard-working/responsible/capable/generous... |
| Can you introduce a little bit about your family? | Yes, of course. There are...people in my family, who are... |

B Complete the following dialogue with your own words.

Li Ming: Hi, Peter! How are you doing these days?

Peter Brown: (1)_____

Li Ming: Fine, thanks. Have you ever lived in an English-speaking country?

Peter Brown: (2)_____

Li Ming: No wonder your English is so good. What do you usually do on weekends?

Peter Brown: (3)_____

Li Ming: I see. Can you introduce a little bit about your family?

Peter Brown: (4)_____

Li Ming: Lucky you! How do you like China so far?

Peter Brown: (5)_____

C Introduce someone in English, such as your best friend or one of your family members.

D Discuss with your partner some Do's and Don'ts when communicating with people from Western countries.

Project   Make a Video of Self-introduction

Make a video to introduce yourself in English within 2 minutes.

UNIT **2**

Weather

Warm-up

Choose the right option to complete the following dialogue.

> A. What a lovely day!
>
> B. cloudy and breezy
>
> C. wear jackets
>
> D. it is autumn
>
> E. I hear that different parts have different weather.

Man: What's the weather like today?

Woman: It's (1)_____. It's not muggy, but very cool.

Man: Yeah. (2)_____

Woman: Yes, isn't it? Why not have a walk by the lake?

Man: Good idea! Let's go.

Man: Please tell me something about the weather in Australia. (3)_____

Woman: Yes, that's right. The weather in our country is quite different from that in China. In Australia, summer is from December to February and winter is from June to August.

Man: Oh, when it's spring in China, (4)_____ in Australia.

Woman: Yes, you're right. And the winter in Sydney is warmer than that in Beijing with rare snow, so people usually (5)_____ in winter.

Man: How do you like the weather in China?

Woman: I like it very much.

Part One Listening

A Listen to the recording and choose the proper response.

1. A. It is good.   B. It is bad.

   C. It is rainy.   D. It is heavy.

2. A. It's five o'clock. B. I got up early.

   C. It is not my fault. D. Yes, it's nice and bright.

3. A. I usually go to bed early. B. It's usually a bit hotter than today.

   C. It's unusually wet today. D. I don't think so.

4. A. Let's turn on the TV. B. It's sunny outside.

   C. Christmas Day. D. Friday.

5. A. You may get one. B. Here you are.

   C. At 9:15. D. It's such a nice change.

B **Listen to the dialogues and choose the best answer to each question.**

1. A. He doesn't believe the weather forecast.

   B. He doesn't like hot weather.

   C. He just bought an air conditioner.

   D. He can fix the woman's air conditioner.

2. A. Take a walk in the rain. B. Delay their outing.

   C. Go on a picnic. D. Call their uncle.

3. A. She doesn't like skating.

   B. She's writing a story about skating.

   C. She's too busy to go skating.

   D. The man shouldn't go skating.

4. A. The woman should wait to buy new clothes.

   B. The cold weather will probably continue.

   C. The weather will warm up soon.

   D. He already has a warm coat.

5. A. The weather yesterday. B. A polluted river.

   C. Hotel accommodations. D. The quality of the air today.

C **Listen to the following dialogue and fill in the blanks with what you hear.**

Mike: What's the weather like in spring?

Amy: It's so (1)_____. Many people have to cover their faces with scarves. They look (2)_____. Besides, people may feel (3)_____ in spring afternoons.

Mike: What's the weather like in summer?

Amy: It's usually hot with (4)_____ in the thirties. Sometimes it's (5)_____. People always meet sudden heavy rain during summer time.

Mike: How is the weather in autumn?

Amy: People are happy to enjoy many (6)_____ days. They like to take boat trips and other outdoor activities in such comfortable weather.

Mike: How's the weather in (7)_____?

Amy: It's (8)_____, but most children like it. They have a good time having snowball fights and making snowmen. But sometimes it's (9)_____. Heavy fog isn't (10)_____ for people.

Part Two 🗼 Reading

Text 1

Does the Weather Actually Affect Your Mood?

There's a common thought around the world that sunny warm weather is **linked** to happiness and cold cloudy weather is linked to sadness. But is there any science behind this idea? Does the weather actually **affect** our biology or is this all in the mind?

Sunlight is our main source of synthesizing[1] vitamin D which is **critical** in producing serotonin[2]. The neurotransmitter[3] is responsible for feeling happy. Low levels of serotonin have been linked to depression[4]. In fact, there is a very real psychological[5] disorder[6] called seasonal[7] affective[8] disorder which **impacts** around 20% of the population, primarily[9] experienced in the darkness of winter. Seasonal affective disorder makes you tired, unmotivated,[10] sad and can make it hard for some people to find reason to get out of bed.

Sunny warm weather has been found to make people more **generous**. Waiters and waitresses report higher tips during warmer weather. Studies have shown that people are more likely to help those in need when it's hot. Romance[11] increases with the temperature. When it's warm, people are more likely to **respond** positively[12] to pick-up **attempts**.

However, warm weather has been found to bring out the worst in people. Studies show that the warmer the temperature is, the more aggressive[13] people will become. The number of violent crimes rises with the temperature. And **peaks** are at about 90 degrees Fahrenheit[14] or 32 degrees Celsius[15]. Late spring and early summer is also in suicide rates peak. Researchers found that outdoor workers were far more likely to **commit** suicide in spring than in winter months. People who worked indoors were far more likely to commit suicide in summer. Studies from both the northern and southern hemisphere[16] report the same seasonal pattern for suicides.

The impact of weather on your mood may depend on your personality[17] type. A 2011 Dutch[18] study on adolescents[19] found that 17% really loved summer. The **subjects** were less angry, less fearful and more positive when the sun was shining. 24% actually hated summer and experienced the exact opposite **effect**. 9% hated rain and felt depressed on gloomy wet days and 48% were not affected by the weather at all.

The impact of the weather on your mood is probably going to be greater in any geographic[20] location[21] that experiences lengthy periods of unusual weather. For instance, if it's hot and sunny for months on end, that's probably going to make more of an impact in Alaska than in Miami.

In any case, there are many **factors** that affect your mood. The weather is an external force that we simply can't control, so try your best not to let it affect your state of mind.

1.（通过化学手段或生物过程）合成　2. 血清素；五羟色胺　3. 神经递质；神经传递素　4. 忧郁，抑郁　5. 心理的；精神上的　6. 失调；紊乱；不适；疾病　7. 季节性的；随季节变化的　8. 感情的，情感的　9. 主要地　10. 动机不明的　11. 浪漫史；爱情关系　12. 积极地　13. 好斗的，挑衅的，富于攻击性的　14. 华氏温度计的；华氏的　15. 摄氏温度计的；摄氏的　16. 半球　17. 个性；性格　18. 荷兰的　19. 青少年　20. 地理的　21. 位置，方位

Vocabulary

link	/lɪŋk/	v.	连接；联合
affect*	/əˈfekt/	v.	影响
critical*	/ˈkrɪtɪkl/	adj.	极重要的；关键的
impact	/ˈɪmpækt/	v.	影响
generous	/ˈdʒenərəs/	adj.	慷慨的，大方的；有雅量的
respond	/rɪˈspɒnd/	v.	回应；对……作出反应
attempt	/əˈtempt/	n.	尝试，试图，企图
peak*	/piːk/	n.	最高点；峰值
commit**	/kəˈmɪt/	v.	做出（错事）；犯罪

subject	/ˈsʌbdʒɪkt/	*n.*	接受试验者，实验对象
effect	/ɪˈfekt/	*n.*	影响；效果
factor	/ˈfæktə(r)/	*n.*	因素，要素

Exercises

A Decide whether the following statements are true (T) or false (F) according to the passage.

(   ) 1. Most people believe that warm weather is related to good mood.

(   ) 2. In winter, people are reluctant to get out of bed only because it is cold.

(   ) 3. People are more likely to give waiters or waitresses tips when it is sunny and warm.

(   ) 4. A 2011 study on adults found that 17% adolescents really loved summer.

(   ) 5. People in Miami instead of Alaska are probably impacted more if it's hot and sunny for months on end.

B Fill in each blank with the proper form of the word given in the brackets.

1. Genetics, lifestyle and diet are all important _____ (factor) in cases of childhood obesity.

2. I can certainly feel the _____ (effect) of too many late nights.

3. Her speech made a profound _____ (impact) on everyone.

4. Your decision is _____ (critic) to our future.

5. The south of the country was worst _____ (affect) by the drought.

C Complete the following sentences in English according to the Chinese.

1. 对于我们的呼吁，公众的反响极为热烈。
   The public have _____ magnificently _____ our appeal.

2. 为削减费用，我们关闭了两家工厂。
   Two factories were closed in an _____ to cut costs.

3. 上午八九点钟之间是交通高峰期。

Traffic reaches its _____ between 8 and 9 in the morning.

4. 受到父母恰当照顾的孩子不太可能犯罪。

Children taken proper care of by their parents are less likely to _____ crimes.

5. 报纸把他的名字与那名歌手联系在一起。

Newspapers have _____ his name _____ the singer.

Text 2

China's 24 Solar Terms

Solar terms, also called *Jieqi* in Chinese, are days marking one of the 24 time buckets of the solar year in traditional Chinese calendar, and were used to indicate the alternation of seasons and climate changes in ancient China. It is a unique component and creative invention of traditional Chinese calendar.

The 24 solar terms each suggest the position of the sun every time it travels 15 degrees on the ecliptic longitude. They include Start of Spring, Rain Water, Awakening of Insects, Spring Equinox, Pure Brightness, Grain Rain, Start of Summer, Grain Buds, Grain in Ear, Summer Solstice, Minor Heat, Major Heat, Start of Autumn, End of Heat, White Dew, Autumn Equinox, Cold Dew, Frost's Descent, Start of Winter, Minor Snow, Major Snow, Winter Solstice, Minor Cold and Major Cold.

China's 24 solar terms were added to the United Nations Educational, Scientific and Cultural Organization's (UNESCO) world intangible cultural heritage list on November 30, 2016. The announcement was made during the 11th session of UNESCO's Intergovernmental Committee for the Safeguarding of Intangible Cultural Heritages in Addis Ababa, Ethiopia's capital.

Origin of 24 Solar Terms

The Yellow River Basin, in northern China, is believed to be the cradle of the solar terms system. Ancient Chinese farmers used astronomical signs, changes in temperature and precipitation as the basis to create the calendar, which was later adopted by multiple ethnic groups in different regions across China.

As early as the Spring and Autumn Period (770–476 BC), Chinese ancestors had already established two major solar terms, *ri nan zhi* (Sun South Most) and *ri bei zhi* (Sun North Most). As of the end of the Warring States Period (453–221 BC), eight key solar terms (Start of Spring,

Spring Equinox, Start of Summer, Summer Solstice, Start of Autumn, Autumn Equinox, Start of Winter and Winter Solstice) marking the four seasons were established according to the different positions of the sun and changes in natural phenomena. The rest of the solar terms were initiated in the Western Han Dynasty (202 BC–8 AD). Hence most terms refer to the climate of Xi'an, capital of the Han Dynasty.

Contemporary Significance

In the current time of technology-based modern farming, traditional solar terms remain relevant. It is also an important cultural existence in modern Chinese social life, serving as a reference in daily life, ancestor worship and others around seasons. Although in modern times it is not regarded as the major guiding knowledge in agriculture production, it remains the symbol of the evolving farming civilization relationship between people and nature. It can recall our memories and remind us that the nature is changing at its own pace. The 24 solar terms are the crystallization of Chinese people in the relationship between human and nature.

This legacy reflects Chinese people's respect for nature and tradition, their unique understanding of the universe, their wisdom to live in harmony with nature, and the world's cultural diversity, said Zhang Ling, an official of the Ministry of Culture, who attended the UNESCO meeting in Addis Ababa.

Exercise

Answer the following questions according to the passage.

1. What are solar terms?

   _____

2. When were solar terms announced as the United Nations Educational, Scientific and Cultural Organization's (UNESCO) world intangible cultural heritage?

   _____

3. Which two solar terms were established during the Spring and Autumn Period?

   _____

4. Can you write down the names of the 24 solar terms?

   _____

5. What is the significance of the 24 solar terms according to Zhang Ling?

   _____

Part Three Writing

A Study the following sample about a weather report.

It's largely cloudy with some patchy rain pushing through southern Scotland, eastern Ireland and eastern regions of Northern Ireland on Wednesday morning. Brighter, fresher weather follows into western Ireland and northwest Scotland during the day. Most of England and much of Wales are to be dry with sunny spells. It is increasingly muggy in England and Wales too as cloud increases in the west and south. An area of thundery rain will be reaching southern England later afternoon and then spreading north through the evening and overnight. Highs could reach 30°C in southeast England, widely 24°C to 27°C, but a much fresher 16°C to 18°C in Scotland, Ireland, northwest England and west Wales.

B Write a weather report with about 100 words, including city names, weather conditions, temperatures, etc.

_____

_____

_____

_____

_____

_____

_____

_____

_____

_____

C Complete the notice according to the Chinese information.

尊敬的客户：

　　因近期受到暴风雪的影响，发往中国北部的包裹可能会出现延迟。我们将持续关注天气状况并作出相应的调整，力争将包裹安全送达。

　　如果您有任何问题，请拨打客服热线 953–3883。感谢您对 ABC 快递公司的信任与支持。

ABC 快递

2021 年 2 月 12 日

Bad Weather Notice: Delays Expected on Northern China Cargo

Dear (1)_____,

　　Recently, (2)_____. As a result, shipments sent to and from this region may experience delays.

　　We will continue to monitor (3)_____ and adjust our resources accordingly. We will strive to deliver your packages safely.

　　(4)_____

　　_____

ABC Express

(5)_____

Part Four 🛥 Speaking

A Read the following sentence patterns concerning weather conditions.

Starter	Response
Which season do you like best? Which is your favorite season?	I like...best because it is always sunny/cool/... I prefer...because I can go fishing / go on a picnic / take a boat trip...
What's the weather like today? How's the weather today? How's the weather in Beijing in summer? What's the weather like in London in winter?	It's sunny/foggy/cloudy...
What does the weather forecast say? What's the weather forecast for tomorrow?	It's going to rain. It's going to be fine tomorrow.
It's a lovely day, isn't it?	Sure. It's...

B Complete the following dialogue with your own words.

Li Ming: Hi, Peter! How are you doing these days?

Peter Brown: (1)_____

Li Ming: Fine, thanks. Beautiful day, isn't it?

Peter Brown: (2)_____

Li Ming: I wish it would stay this way for the weekend.

Peter Brown: (3)_____

Li Ming: What does the weather forecast say?

Peter Brown: (4)_____

Li Ming: Great! I plan to fly a kite. Would you like to go with me?

Peter Brown: (5)_____

C Introduce the weather conditions in your hometown in English.

D Discuss the reasons why people from Western countries, especially the U.K., like to talk about weather.

Project · Make a Speech on the Weather of Your Hometown or Your Favorite Place

Make a speech on the weather of your hometown or your favorite place from the aspects of temperature, humidity, wind strength, etc.

UNIT **3**

Learning

Warm-up

Choose the right option to complete the following dialogue.

> A. Glad to see you, Allen.
>
> B. I really take a strong interest in IoT.
>
> C. What's your major?
>
> D. I've heard that this major has good career prospects.
>
> E. What do you want to do after graduation?

Allen: Hi, nice to see you, Linda.

Linda: (1)_____

Allen: Where are you going?

Linda: I'm going to the library to borrow some books related to my major.

Allen: (2)_____

Linda: Internet of Things, simplified as IoT.

Allen: Wow, it is becoming more and more popular these years.

Linda: Yes, it is.

Allen: (3)_____

Linda: Do you mean my future job hunting is easy?

Allen: Yes, that's right.

Linda: I hope so.

Allen: (4)_____

Linda: I dream of being admitted to one of China's top 500 companies, such as Huawei, Alibaba and so on.

Allen: Wow, sounds great!

Linda: (5)_____ So I wish I could take up a new job closely related to my major.

Allen: I can't agree with you more.

Part One  Listening

Ⓐ Listen to the recording and choose the proper response.

1. A. About 150 pages.　　　　B. It is very long.
   C. About one year.　　　　 D. It is very short.

2. A. It's popular.　　　　　 B. Internet of Things.
   C. Yes, I like it.　　　　　 D. I learn it well.

3. A. We should know how to learn.
   B. No, I don't like it.
   C. There are a lot of learning patterns.
   D. Online learning.

4. A. No problem.　　　　　 B. What is it?
   C. Sorry, I don't know.　　 D. Yes, I could.

5. A. I have made a monthly study plan.
   B. Yes, of course, what would you like to know?
   C. You have the right.
   D. You are welcome.

Ⓑ Listen to the dialogues and choose the best answer to each question.

1. A. Quite a few years.　　　B. Two months.
   C. Almost three months.　 D. Four months.

2. A. Every day.
   B. Every day except Thursday.
   C. Monday, Wednesday and Friday.
   D. Monday, Tuesday and Friday.

3. A. Larry usually gets good grades.
   B. He helped Larry write the report.
   C. He's surprised at Larry's grade.
   D. It's strange that Larry and Mark are lab partners.

4. A. A smooth surface.　　　B. An apartment.
   C. An actor.　　　　　　　D. A movie.

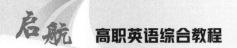

5. A. They're going to France for a vacation.

   B. The woman doesn't need to study now.

   C. He's concerned about the woman's study.

   D. The woman isn't worrying about her vacation.

C **Listen to the following dialogue and fill in the blanks with what you hear.**

Tim: Hi, Jane. What do you think of today's class meeting?

Jane: How (1)_____! The head teacher encourages us to set three (2)_____ goals in college and work at them.

Tim: Yes, exactly! Three years in college will be gone in a flash. We really can't (3)_____ to waste time.

Jane: Have you had phased goals so far?

Tim: I'm still at sea. How about you?

Jane: Well, in the first year I want to completely know my major and figure out what I am good at. In the second year, I should learn my major courses well in (4)_____ for my following internship. In the last year, I hope I can go to a good company to get a good (5)_____.

Tim: Wow, sounds great! You are really my role model.

Jane: Thanks.

Tim: By the way, I don't know how to (6)_____ these goals because I'm a lazy man.

Jane: Uh...I think the only way to (7)_____ your laziness is to learn to manage your time. You know, good time (8)_____ can guard against procrastination.

Tim: Yes, you're right! Next, I will figure out what I want and then make a tight time (9)_____ to finish it.

Jane: Great! Let's work hard together!

Tim: I believe we will achieve (10)_____ three years later.

Part Two   Reading

Text 1

Ways to Manage Your Time

It might not be your cup of tea, but sticking to a daily plan is the only **sensible** way to **achieve** goals. Try it, and you might like it.

Step 1: Write It down

Draw columns on a sheet of paper to **track** activities, time devoted to each, and sudden emergencies[1]. Document a normal day to determine which activities go as planned and what **delays** as a result of **interruptions**.

Make a daily to-do list that prioritizes[2] your tasks, so you know which are the most important.

Step 2: Guard Against Procrastination[3]

Guard against procrastination by sticking to the new **schedule** no matter what happens. Detail action steps to better streamline[4] activities, delegate[5] some responsibilities, group some tasks, or eliminate[6] diversions[7].

Step 3: Get Away from Distractions

Choose a place free from **distraction** and stay on task. Let everyone know this time is sacred[8] and that you are not to be disturbed.

Avoid checking email all day—a habitual distraction that loses time. Check only at certain times throughout the day as part of the **overall** plan.

Step 4: Limit Multitasking[9]

Limit multitasking to **maintain** focus. Finish the job at hand before moving to the next.

Step 5: Reserve Time to Review and Plan

Reserve an hour or two each week to **review** assignments, notes, and your schedule. **Adapt** the phased or long-term goals to new **challenges**. Whether you're a student or an office worker, better time **management** will help you reach those lofty[10] goals!

---

1. 紧急事件   2. 按优先顺序列出   3. 拖延症   4. 使简单化；使合理化   5. 委派   6. 消除   7. 分散注意力的事   8. 神圣的   9. 多重任务处理   10. 崇高的

⛵ Vocabulary

sensible*	/'sensəbl/	*adj.*	合理的；明智的
achieve	/ə'tʃiːv/	*v.*	实现；获得
track	/træk/	*v.*	追踪，跟踪
delay	/dɪ'leɪ/	*v.*	耽搁，延误
interruption*	/ˌɪntə'rʌpʃn/	*n.*	干扰，中断
schedule	/'ʃedjuːl/	*n.*	计划表；时间表
distraction**	/dɪ'strækʃn/	*n.*	分心的事物；干扰
overall	/ˌəuvə'rɔːl/	*adj.*	整体的；全部的
maintain	/meɪn'teɪn/	*v.*	维持，保持
reserve**	/rɪ'zɜːv/	*v.*	预留
review	/rɪ'vjuː/	*v.*	回顾；复习
adapt	/ə'dæpt/	*v.*	（使）适应
challenge	/'tʃælɪndʒ/	*n.*	挑战
management	/'mænɪdʒmənt/	*n.*	管理

⛵ Exercises

Ⓐ Decide whether the following statements are true (T) or false (F) according to the passage.

(　　) *1.* You can write down what you should do on the list and then allocate the same amount of time to your tasks.

(　　) *2.* Sticking to a new schedule helps avoid your procrastination.

(　　) *3.* If you want to finish a task, you'd better choose a place free from distraction.

(　　) *4.* Multitasking helps you maintain your focus.

(　　) *5.* Reserving time to review and plan is also a good way to manage your time.

Ⓑ Fill in each blank with the proper form of the word given in the brackets.

1. Now most freshmen have _____ (adapt) to the new school life.

2. The prescription of drugs is a doctor's _____ (responsible).

3. A good resume should include your good skills and the _____ (achieve) you've made.

4. Teaching young children is a _____ (challenge) but rewarding job.

5. We shouldn't _____ (distraction) our attention in class.

C **Complete the following sentences in English according to the Chinese.**

1. 这一路段推迟到九月份启用。
    The opening of this section of the road is _____ until September.

2. 我们在这儿谈话不会被打断。
    We can talk here without _____.

3. 很多事情都要取决于和顾客建立并保持良好的关系。
    A lot of things depend on building and _____ a good relationship with customers.

4. 这里有一个房间专门留给吸烟者用。
    Here is a separate room _____ for smokers.

5. 这个大学开设了许多时间管理方面的课程。
    The university has opened a lot of courses on time _____.

Text ②

Learning, Chinese-style

For a month in the spring of 1987, my wife Ellen and I lived in the bustling eastern Chinese city of Nanjing with our 18-month-old son Benjamin while studying arts education in Chinese kindergartens and elementary schools. But one of the most telling lessons Ellen and I got in the difference between Chinese and American ideas of education came not in the classroom but in the lobby of the Jinling Hotel where we stayed in Nanjing. The key to our room was attached to a large plastic block with the room number on it. Benjamin loved to carry the key around, shaking it vigorously. He also liked to try to place it into the slot. Because of his tender age and incomplete understanding of the need to position the key, he would usually fail.

Now both Ellen and I were perfectly happy to allow Benjamin to bang the key near the key slot. His exploratory behavior seemed harmless enough. But I soon observed an interesting phenomenon. Any Chinese staff member nearby would come over to watch Benjamin and, noting his lack of initial success, attempt to assist. He or she would hold onto Benjamin's hand and, gently but firmly, guide it directly toward the slot, reposition it as necessary, and help him to insert it. The "teacher" would then smile somewhat expectantly at Ellen or me, as if awaiting a thank you—and on occasion would frown slightly, as if considering us to be neglecting our parental duties.

I soon realized that this incident was directly relevant to our assigned tasks in China: to investigate the ways of early childhood education (especially in arts), and to throw light on Chinese attitudes toward creativity. In terms of attitudes towards creativity there seems to be a reversal of priorities: young Westerners making their boldest departures first and then gradually mastering the tradition; and young Chinese being almost inseparable from the tradition, but, over time, possibly evolving to a point equally original.

However, I do not want to overstate my case. There is enormous creativity to be found in Chinese scientific, technological and artistic innovations past and present. And there is a danger of exaggerating creative breakthroughs in the West. When any innovation is examined closely, its reliance on previous achievements is all too apparent (the "standing on the shoulders of giants" phenomenon).

But assuming that the contrast I have developed is valid, and that the fostering of skills and creativity are both worthwhile goals, the important question becomes this: Can we gather, from the Chinese and American extremes, a superior way to approach education, perhaps striking a better balance between the poles of creativity and basic skills?

Exercise

Answer the following questions according to the passage.

1. What were the author and his wife doing in Nanjing in the spring of 1987?

   _____

2. How would Chinese staff members of the hotel respond to Benjamin's attempt to place the key into the slot?

   _____

3. What are the different attitudes towards creativity between Chinese people and Americans?

   _____

4. What's the function of the question in the last paragraph?

   _____

5. What do you think of Chinese learning style and American learning style?

_____

Part Three Writing

Ⓐ **Study the following sample about a study plan.**

Monthly Study Plan		
Goals	**1st month**	**2nd month**
	• to get up early to recite English words • to develop a good learning habit	• to exchange learning experience with seniors • to know different kinds of competitions
Goals	**3rd month**	**4th month**
	• to assess learning effects • to take part in different kinds of competitions • to prepare for CET-4 examination	• to go over all the lessons • to try my best to get a scholarship • to read some extracurricular books
Goals	**5th month**	**6th month**
	• to preview major courses • to take notes of different courses • to prepare for social practice activities	• to take part in some association activities • to take part in English Corner • to master practical skills related to major courses
Goals	**7th month**	**8th month**
	• to adjust learning strategies • to assess learning effects • to prepare for Computer Rank Examination	• to go over all the lessons • to try my best to get a scholarship • to prepare for CET-6 examination

B Evaluate the study plan in Exercise A.

Strengths: _____

_____

_____

_____

_____

Weaknesses: _____

_____

_____

_____

_____

C Complete the letter of congratulation according to the Chinese information.

李明在 2020 年全国大学生英语竞赛中获得一等奖，这是他所在学校学生迄今为止在此项大赛中取得的最好成绩。请以 James 的名义给他写一封祝贺信，并祝愿他在英语学习上取得更大的成功。

写信日期：2020 年 11 月 9 日

(1)_____

Dear Li Ming,

Allow me to convey my warmest (2)_____ on your obtaining the First Prize in 2020 National English Contest for College Students.

Undoubtedly, owing to your own efforts, you have made great achievements in English study. I was delighted to learn that so far nobody else on the campus made (3)_____ in this contest than you did. You are really something.

I sincerely hope you will make even greater (4)_____ in English study in the future.

(5)_____

James

Part Four 🏛 Speaking

Ⓐ **Read the following sentence patterns concerning learning.**

Starter	Response
What's your major?	Internet of Things / Cloud Computing / Software Technology / Electronic Information Technology / Network Technology...
What courses are you studying?	Fundamentals of Electric Circuits / C Language Programming / Sensor Detection and Application...
Do you know what blended learning is?	Yes, blended learning is the combination of classroom learning and online learning.
Do you have a long-term goal?	Yes, my long-term goal is to go to a new college for further education....
What should you do to achieve your long-term goals?	I should make a good study plan and manage my time well.
What do you want to do after graduation?	I dream of...after graduation.

B Complete the following dialogue with your own words.

Tom: Hi, Jenny. Glad to meet you.

Jenny: Glad to meet you too, Tom. We are classmates now.

Tom: Yes, I hope we can help each other with the study of our major courses.

Jenny: Yeah, of course.

Tom: How much do you know about our major—IoT? Is it difficult to learn the courses related to it?

Jenny: Well, you have got me there. (1)_____. Some students think it is really difficult to learn the courses, but others consider it easy to learn them.

Tom: (2) _____?

Jenny: Uh...in my opinion, it is not very hard to learn these courses. We must master good learning strategies and methods.

Tom: I can't agree with you more. You reap what you sow. (3)_____ _____?

Jenny: Of course. First, you should keep focused in class and need timely review. What's more, you'd better consult the teacher about what you can't understand. Most importantly, you're supposed to (4)_____.

Tom: Yes, you said it.

Jenny: But please remember you should assess your learning effects regularly according to your weekly study plan.

Tom: Right! Once learning effects are not good, we should adjust our learning strategies and methods. Right?

Jenny: Yes, you're absolutely right.

Tom: (5)_____, Jenny.

Jenny: You are welcome.

C Introduce your major in English, including the name, compulsory courses, learning strategies, career prospect, etc.

D Discuss with your partner the effective ways of learning English.

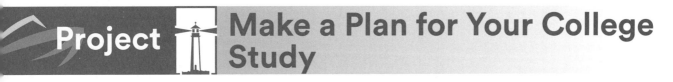

Project Make a Plan for Your College Study

Make a plan for your college study as specifically as you can.

My Plan for College Study

Long-term goal	
Phased goals	Grade 1: Grade 2: Grade 3:

College Study Plan

UNIT **4**

Health

Warm-up

Choose the right option to complete the following dialogue.

> A. What time is convenient for you?
>
> B. I haven't got much sleep.
>
> C. What's wrong with you exactly?
>
> D. make an appointment
>
> E. I've got a temperature too.

Nurse: Hello, this is Dr. Smith's office. How can I help you?

Li Ming: I don't feel well. Can I (1)_____ to see the doctor?

hospital

Nurse: Certainly! What's your name, please?

Li Ming: Li Ming.

Nurse: And your date of birth?

Li Ming: December 20, 2001.

Nurse: OK. I've put down your information. (2)_____

Li Ming: I had a sore throat and a bad headache since last night. (3)_____

Nurse: I see. Dr. Smith is available on Tuesday afternoon at 4 o'clock, Wednesday morning at 10 o'clock, and Friday afternoon at 1 o'clock. (4)_____

Li Ming: I'm afraid (5)_____ So I would like to see the doctor as soon as possible.

Nurse: Alright, that's fine. Let me make your appointment on Tuesday afternoon at 4 o'clock with Dr. Smith.

Li Ming: OK. Thank you very much.

Nurse: You are welcome. Bye.

Li Ming: Bye.

Part One 🗼 Listening

A Listen to the recording and choose the proper response.

1. A. I like English. B. I live in China.
   C. I have a bad headache. D. I am 18.

2. A. Thanks, but I am on a diet. B. No, it tastes bad.
   C. Sorry, I am late. D. OK, I like chocolates.

3. A. For a week. B. Since tomorrow.
   C. Twice a day. D. In the evening.

4. A. Sorry. B. Thank you.
   C. Excuse me. D. Oh, no.

5. A. Music. B. Movie.
   C. Soccer. D. Book.

B Listen to the dialogues and choose the best answer to each question.

1. A. Before meals. B. After meals.
   C. Before going to bed. D. After getting up.

2. A. She'll have it filled. B. It started hurting last Sunday.
   C. It never hurts. D. It had never been filled.

3. A. Lose five pounds. B. Gain ten more pounds.
   C. Buy some new clothes. D. Gain five more pounds.

4. A. She was on vacation.

   B. She was working for another company.

   C. She was sick.

   D. She was attending a meeting.

5. A. Candy. B. Cigarettes.
   C. Toys. D. Books.

C Listen to the following dialogue and fill in the blanks with what you hear.

Patient: Good morning, doctor!

Doctor: Good morning! (1)_____, please. What's the matter?

Patient: Well, I don't (2)_____. I feel cold and shivery. Also, I have a bad headache and (3)_____.

Doctor: How long have you been like this?

Patient: Since (4)_____. I didn't get a good night's sleep.

Doctor: Let me look at your (5)_____ first. Please open your mouth and say "ah".

Patient: Ah…

Doctor: Now, let me take your (6)_____. Please put the point of this thermometer under your (7)_____.

(Five minutes later.)

Patient: Do I have a temperature?

Doctor: Yes, you have (8)_____. You've caught a bad cold.

Patient: Is it serious? I have a lot of work to do. I don't have time to be sick.

Doctor: Not really. I want you to put aside your work for a while and have (9)_____. Take this medicine (10)_____. Don't worry. You'll be fine very soon.

Part Two 🗼 Reading

Text 1

The Food Pyramid: Healthy or Not

The food pyramid[1], created by the U.S. Department of Agriculture (USDA), debuted[2] in 1992. It **recommends** the number of servings[3] of each food group a person should eat each day to stay healthy.

But in recent years, doctors and scientists have studied the food pyramid and have begun to question just how helpful and healthful the **guidelines** really are. In fact, the USDA itself is reevaluating the food pyramid.

The food pyramid **indicates** that people should eat between 6 and 11 servings of **grains** a day. Grains include bread, pasta and cereals[4]. One serving equals one slice of bread or a cup of cooked rice or pasta. By recommending so many grain products, which are usually low in fat, the USDA has been **promoting** a low-fat diet.

But many experts now believe that a low-fat diet that's high in sugar (most processed grains, such as white flour, are made out of forms of sugar like glucose[5] and fructose[6]) has actually led to an increase in obesity[7] and heart problems.

Some doctors now contend[8] that a diet higher in fat—with the fat coming from nuts, cheeses, some oils (such as olive[9] oil), poultry[10], eggs and lean meat—will keep people trimmer[11] and healthier than a high-carbohydrate[12], low-fat diet.

So what should you eat? Eat a variety of foods from all five food groups—grains, vegetables, fruit, **dairy** (milk, **yoghurt** and cheese) and fats and oils. But when eating grains, try to avoid white bread and pasta and instead eat whole-grain foods, such as whole-wheat bread, oatmeal[13] and whole-wheat pasta. They contain more natural **nutrients** and are high in **fiber**. Fiber helps to lower cholesterol[14] and may protect against some cancers.

Try to eat less red meat, such as hamburgers and steak, and eat more fish, nuts and cheese. You won't go wrong eating lots of fruits and vegetables. No one is questioning their nutritional value. In fact, many vegetables have been found to reduce the **risk** of getting cancer, and fruits are a great **source** of many **vitamins**, such as vitamin C.

Although most junk foods[15] taste great, they provide little or no nutritional value. Sodas have lots of sugar and few nutrients. Many also contain caffeine[16]. Cakes and cookies contain lots of sugar and fat and not very many vitamins and **minerals**. Potato chips are high in fat and salt. Instead, choose healthy **snacks**, such as fruit, nuts and yogurt.

---

1. 金字塔　2. 首次公布　3.（食品等的）一份　4. 谷类　5. 葡萄糖　6. 果糖　7. 肥胖症　8. 认为　9. 橄榄　10. 家禽肉　11. 身材苗条的　12. 碳水化合物　13. 燕麦片　14. 胆固醇　15. 垃圾食品　16. 咖啡因

Vocabulary

recommend	/ˌrekə'mend/	v.	推荐，举荐；介绍
guideline	/'gaɪdlaɪn/	n.	指导方针；准则
indicate	/'ɪndɪkeɪt/	v.	表明；显示
grain**	/greɪn/	n.	谷物，谷粒
promote	/prə'məʊt/	v.	促进；推动

dairy	/'deəri/	n.	乳制品
yoghurt*	/'jɒgət/	n.	酸奶
nutrient**	/'njuːtriənt/	n.	营养素，营养物
fiber**	/'faɪbə(r)/	n.	（食物中的）纤维素
risk	/rɪsk/	n.	危险，风险
source	/sɔːs/	n.	来源，出处
vitamin*	/'vɪtəmɪn/	n.	维生素
mineral*	/'mɪnərəl/	n.	矿物质；矿物
snack	/snæk/	n.	零食；小吃；快餐

Exercises

A Decide whether the following statements are true (T) or false (F) according to the passage.

(　　) *1.* The food pyramid was proposed by American scientists in the 21st century.

(　　) *2.* The authority of the guidelines has never been challenged.

(　　) *3.* Whole-wheat foods contain more natural nutrients and are higher in fiber.

(　　) *4.* Fruits are a great source of many vitamins.

(　　) *5.* Tasty foods, such as potato chips, are recommended by the author.

B Fill in each blank with the proper form of the word given in the brackets.

1. Her job is mainly concerned with sales and _____ (promote).

2. The effectiveness of the vaccine against COVID-19 has been _____ (evaluate) by many organizations around the world.

3. The committee made _____ (recommend) to raise the workers' pay.

4. It is _____ (risk) to cross the street without using the zebra crossing.

5. There are clear _____ (indicate) that the economy is improving.

C Complete the following sentences in English according to the Chinese.

1. 研究显示，饮食习惯正迅速改变。
   Research _____ that eating habits are changing fast.

2. 她工作勤奋，不久就得到提升了。
   She worked hard and was soon _____.

3. 他冒着生命危险去救她。
   He _____ to save her.

4. 请给我来杯矿泉水。
   A glass of _____, please.

5. 乳制品可能会引起某些人的过敏反应。
   _____ may provoke allergic reactions in some people.

Text 2

TCM Wins New Global Acceptance

Traditional Chinese medicine (TCM) isn't supported by most Westerners. However, this is starting to change.

TCM has been included in the new version of the International Classification of Diseases (ICD), which was published by the World Health Organization in 2019, *Nature* magazine reported.

It was the first time for TCM to be included in the ICD, which served as "the international standard for diseases and health conditions", according to *China Daily*.

Ryan Abbott at the Center for East-West Medicine at the University of California, Los Angeles, U.S., said this could benefit TCM.

The inclusion of TCM in the ICD "is a mainstream acceptance that will have significant impact around the world", Abbott told *Nature*.

TCM has seen some growth in other countries, with a number of famous people being known to use it. For example, during the 2016 Rio Olympic Games, U.S. swimmer Michael Phelps was seen with circular bruises on his body. The bruises were caused by cupping, a traditional Chinese medicinal practice that has been around for more than 2,000 years.

In 2015, Chinese scientist Tu Youyou was awarded the Nobel Prize in Physiology or

Medicine for her discovery of artemisinin, a drug that can cure malaria. She said she was inspired by TCM.

China has made some efforts to promote TCM overseas. Twenty-six TCM centers were set up overseas over three years, according to a 2017 report published by Xinhua News Agency.

TCM still faces many challenges, such as a lack of clinical evidence as to how it works precisely, according to *China Daily*. "Not subject to Western testing standards such as randomized controlled clinical trials…TCM's effectiveness has been difficult to study or provide evidence for," according to CNN.

Some say that TCM methodology should be combined with modern scientific methods to make it more acceptable to people outside of China.

"Tried and tested over thousands of years, the effectiveness of TCM is clear," Lu Chuanjian, vice-president of the Guangdong Provincial Hospital of Chinese Medicine, told *China Daily*.

"Now we need to use modern technology and ways of thinking to explain to the world how TCM works on specific diseases and [to] prove that it can cure diseases," Lu added.

Exercise

Answer the following questions according to the passage.

1. What is the new global acceptance of TCM?

   _____

2. What did Ryan Abbott tell *Nature*?

   _____

3. Are there any famous people using TCM in the world?

   _____

4. When was TCM first practiced?

   _____

5. What achievements has China made while promoting TCM overseas?

   _____

Part Three　Writing

A Study the following sample about ways of keeping healthy.

Health is the most important element in our lives. Without health, it is meaningless to be wealthy or successful. So how should we keep healthy?

In my opinion, a balanced diet is the secret of staying healthy. Chinese Balance Dietary Pagoda shows us the kinds and amount of food that we need every day. To keep fit, we need about 500 grams of rice, cereal or potatoes, 500 grams of vegetables, one fruit, one egg, 100 grams of fish, meat or poultry, a glass of milk, some nuts, a little oil and salt, and 7 glasses of water each day. Remember to have our breakfast like a king, lunch like a prince, and supper like a pauper.

Of course a balanced diet is not enough to keep us healthy. It is also important for us to take moderate exercise, keep a healthy lifestyle, and maintain a good mood.

B Write down your suggestions on keeping healthy with about 150 words.

_____

_____

_____

_____

_____

_____

_____

_____

_____

_____

_____

C Complete the leave application according to the Chinese information.

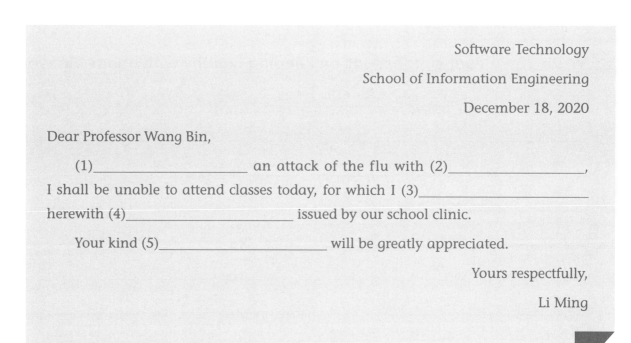

王斌教授：

因患感冒，头痛剧烈，今天不能前来上课，特附上医务室所出诊断书，请准假为感。

李明

信息工程学院软件技术专业

2020 年 12 月 18 日

Software Technology

School of Information Engineering

December 18, 2020

Dear Professor Wang Bin,

(1)_____ an attack of the flu with (2)_____, I shall be unable to attend classes today, for which I (3)_____ herewith (4)_____ issued by our school clinic.

Your kind (5)_____ will be greatly appreciated.

Yours respectfully,

Li Ming

Part Four 🗼 Speaking

A Read the following sentence patterns concerning seeing a doctor.

Starter	Response
What's wrong with you?	I feel… / I have a sore throat…
May I have your name / phone number…?	Yes, I'm… / my phone number is…
Which department do you want to register with?	I want to see a surgeon/physician/ pediatrician…
What time is convenient for you?	I think I would be fine on…
How long have you been like this?	I didn't feel well since…
Are there any other symptoms?	Yes, I have a runny nose / bad headache…
What did you have last night?	I had…for supper.

B Complete the following dialogue with your own words.

Doctor: Good morning! What is bothering you?

Patient: (1)_____

Doctor: How long have you been like this?

Patient: (2)_____

Doctor: What did you have for supper?

Patient: (3)_____

Doctor: No appetite, vomiting, no energy. These are symptoms of food poisoning.

Patient: (4)_____

Doctor: Don't worry. You'll be fine. Take this medicine twice a day, drink plenty of water and have a good rest.

Patient: (5)_____

C Talk about some common diseases and their symptoms in English.

D Discuss your understanding of health with a partner.

Project Introduce Ways of Keeping Healthy

Make a presentation on how to keep healthy within 2 minutes using PowerPoint slides.

UNIT **5**

Food

Warm-up

Choose the right option to complete the following dialogue.

> A. May I have your name
>
> B. Would that be OK?
>
> C. I'd like to reserve a table for three
>
> D. What can I do for you
>
> E. At what time

Waitress: This is Britannia Fish Restaurant.
(1)_____, sir?

Lin Fei: (2)_____ on Saturday evening this week, and I'd like to have a table near the window facing the Thames. (3)_____

Waitress: Certainly, sir. (4)_____, please?

Lin Fei: Yes, my name is Lin Fei.

Waitress: OK, Mr. Lin...a table for three...Saturday evening. (5)_____, sir?

Lin Fei: 7:30. Is that OK?

Waitress: Yes, thank you for calling, sir. See you then.

Part One  Listening

Ⓐ Listen to the recording and choose the proper response.

1. A. I like coffee very much.   B. I don't like drinking tea.
    C. Coffee, please.   D. Hold on, please.

2. A. I'm sorry to hear that.   B. No, nothing special.
    C. My pleasure.   D. Me, too.

3. A. Fantastic.   B. I like Chinese cuisines.

C. Huaiyang cuisine is my favorite.   D. Sorry, I know little.

4. A. I don't know how to make it.   B. Medium well.

   C. Wait a minute.   D. I like eating steak.

5. A. For what time, sir?   B. Here it is.

   C. Hello, Huijin Restaurant.   D. Can I help you?

B **Listen to the dialogues and choose the best answer to each question.**

1. A. She'd rather take a break later.

   B. She likes the suggestion very much.

   C. She never drinks soda.

   D. She doesn't think he's serious.

2. A. He likes Mexican food.

   B. He was expecting a better dinner.

   C. The dinner was expensive.

   D. He enjoyed the food more than the woman did.

3. A. Concert.   B. Hotel.

   C. Bank.   D. Restaurant.

4. A. She'll sell him a cup of coffee.   B. The coffee cup's too full.

   C. She'd like some coffee.   D. Coffee's hard on her nerves.

5. A. At a restaurant.   B. At a bank.

   C. At a hotel.   D. At a friend's house.

C **Listen to the following dialogue and fill in the blanks with what you hear.**

Secretary: Come this way, please. Mrs. Golden, our general manager is (1)_____ you. ...This is Mr. Jiang Min, general manager of the China National Light Industrial Products Import Corporation.

Mrs. Golden: How do you do? Mr. Jiang. I'm very pleased to have the (2)_____ to meet you.

Mr. Jiang: How do you do? Mrs. Golden. Welcome to this party in your (3)_____. Did you have a nice trip?

Mrs. Golden: Yes, it was very (4)_____. Thank you.

Mr. Jiang: Take a seat, please.

Mrs. Golden: Thank you! Thank you very much for arranging such a (5)_____ dinner for me.

Mr. Jiang: It's our (6)_____. What would you like to drink, Maotai or whisky?

Mrs. Golden: Maotai is pretty (7)_____, isn't it?

Mr. Jiang: Yes, but it is the best (8)_____ in China. Would you like a try?

Mrs. Golden: Let me have a little.

Mr. Jiang: Let me propose a (9)_____ to your health.

Mrs. Golden: Thank you very much. And allow me to propose a toast to a good beginning to our (10)_____.

Part Two   Reading

Text 1

Aspects of English Life: Meals of a Day

The **traditional** English breakfast—tea, toast, **jam**, eggs, **bacon**, **sausages**, tomatoes, mushrooms, etc.—is both good and filling, and breakfast is the only **aspect** of English cooking that is **frequently** and enthusiastically[1] praised by **foreigners**. Few of the English eat this **regularly**. The **upper**-middle and upper classes drink weak, dishwater-colored, unsweetened[2] tea. Taking tea with sugar is regarded by many as an infallible[3] lower class indicator[4]. Putting the milk into the cup first is also a lower-class habit. Toast is a breakfast staple[5], and an all-purpose, anytime **comfort** food. Margarine[6] is **regarded** as decidedly "common by the middle and upper classes, who use **butter**.

The English do not take the middle-of-the-day meal at all seriously: Most make do with a sandwich or some other quick, easy, single-dish meal. The timing of lunch is not a class indicator, as almost everyone has lunch at around one o'clock. The only class indicator is what you call this meal: If you call it "dinner", you are working class; everyone else, from the lower-middles upwards, calls it "lunch".

The evening meal is a clear class indicator: If you call it "tea" and eat it at around half past six, you are almost working class or of working-class **origin**. If you call it "dinner", and eat it at around seven, you are probably lower-middle or middle-middle. If you normally only use the term "dinner" for rather more formal evening meals, and call your **informal** family evening meal "supper", you are probably upper-middle or upper class. The timing of these meals tends to be more flexible[7], but a family "supper" is generally eaten at around half past seven, while a "dinner" would usually be later, from half past eight onwards.

To everyone but the working classes, "tea" is a light meal taken at around four in the afternoon, and consists of tea with cakes, scones[8], jam, **biscuits** and perhaps a little sandwiches—traditionally including cucumber[9] sandwiches—with the crusts[10] cut off. The working classes call this "afternoon tea", to distinguish[11] it from the evening "tea" that the rest call "supper" or "dinner".

---

1. 热情地　2. 未加糖的　3. 确切的，绝无错误的　4. 标志　5. 主食　6. 人造奶油　7. 灵活的　8. 烤饼
9. 黄瓜　10. 外皮，外壳　11. 区别

Vocabulary

traditional	/trəˈdɪʃənl/	*adj.*	传统的
jam	/dʒæm/	*n.*	果酱
bacon	/ˈbeɪkən/	*n.*	熏猪肉；培根肉
sausage	/ˈsɒsɪdʒ/	*n.*	香肠
aspect	/ˈæspekt/	*n.*	方面
frequently	/ˈfriːkwəntli/	*adv.*	频繁地
foreigner	/ˈfɒrənə(r)/	*n.*	外国人
regularly	/ˈregjələli/	*adv.*	有规律地
upper	/ˈʌpə(r)/	*adj.*	上等的；上面的
comfort*	/ˈkʌmfət/	*n.*	舒适，安慰
regard	/rɪˈgɑːd/	*v.*	把……看作
butter	/ˈbʌtə(r)/	*n.*	黄油
origin**	/ˈɒrɪdʒɪn/	*n.*	起源
informal*	/ɪnˈfɔːml/	*adj.*	不正式的
biscuit	/ˈbɪskɪt/	*n.*	饼干

Exercises

A Decide whether the following statements are true (T) or false (F) according to the passage.

(   ) *1.* English breakfast is frequently praised by many foreigners.

(   ) *2.* Taking tea with sugar is a habit of English upper classes.

(   ) *3.* Englishmen care about their lunch very much.

(   ) *4.* Upper classes usually call the evening meal "supper".

(   ) *5.* The time of the meals is fixed for Englishmen.

B Fill in each blank with the proper form of the word given in the brackets.

1. By _____ (traditional), it's the bride's parents who pay for the wedding.

2. Her headaches are becoming less _____ (frequently).

3. _____ (regularly) exercise is beneficial to our physical health.

4. Joyce has a _____ (comfort) apartment in Portland.

5. Tom was widely _____ (regard) as the most rigid student in class.

C Complete the following sentences in English according to the Chinese.

1. 做煎饼时，你最好在上面放上一根香肠和几片培根肉。
When making a pancake, you'd better put a _____ and some pieces of _____ on its top.

2. 与人打交道是我工作中最重要的一个方面。
Dealing with people is the most important _____ of my work.

3. 我们的黄油大多产自新西兰。
Much of our _____ comes from New Zealand.

4. 这一传统源于中世纪。
The tradition has its _____ in the Middle Ages.

5. 董事会成员预计在今天稍后进行非正式讨论。
Board members are due to have _____ discussions later on today.

Text 2

Huaiyang Cuisine

Huaiyang cuisine originated from the Pre-Qin Period (before 221BC), became famous during the Sui (581–618) and Tang (618–907) Dynasties, and was recognized as a distinct regional style during the Ming (1368–1644) and Qing (1636–1912) Dynasties. This cuisine includes dishes from Yangzhou, Huai'an, Suzhou and Shanghai.

Raw materials of Huaiyang dishes include fresh and live aquatic products. The carving techniques are delicate, of which the melon carving technique is especially well-known. The flavor of Huaiyang cuisine is light, fresh and sweet. If Shandong cuisine is characterized by stirring and frying over a hot fire, Huaiyang cuisine is characterized by stewing, braising, and steaming over a low fire for a long time. Famous dishes cooked this way are chicken braised with chestnuts, pork steamed in lotus leaf, duck stewed with eight treasures, meatballs with crab meat in Yangzhou style, and butterfly-shaped sea cucumber (sea cucumber cut into butterfly shapes and cooked with flavorings). Other famous dishes include stewed crab with clear soup, crystal meat, sweet and sour mandarin fish, sauteed eel shreds and so on. The vegetarian banquet is a special feature of Huaiyang cuisine, and the vegetarian dishes in Beijing cuisine are mostly variants of Huaiyang cuisine.

Huaiyang snacks and refreshments are exquisite, such as boiled shredded dried bean curd, steamed dumplings with minced meat and gravy and so on.

Exercise

Answer the following questions according to the passage.

1. Which dynasty did Huaiyang cuisine originate from?

   _____

2. What raw materials does Huaiyang cuisine have?

   _____

3. What is the flavor of Huaiyang cuisine?

   _____

4. Can you list some famous Huaiyang dishes?

   _____

5. What do you think of Huaiyang snacks?

_____

Part Three 🔦 Writing

A Study the following sample about making scrambled eggs with tomatoes.

Step 1: Prepare two tomatoes and two eggs, which are the main ingredients of this dish.

Step 2: Remove the stalk (梗) from the tomatoes and cut them into pieces.

Step 3: Stir (搅拌) the eggs into a blend.

Step 4: Put some oil into the pan and pour the egg mixture into the pan after the oil heats up.

Step 5: Stir-fry (翻炒) the eggs, mash (捣碎) them into small pieces with the spatula (锅铲) and put them into a plate.

Step 6: Pour in a little oil, put tomatoes into the pan and stir-fry them.

Step 7: Change the hot fire into a low fire when tomatoes get soft, add proper salt and sugar and continue stir-frying.

Step 8: Put the fried eggs into the pan again and stir-fry quickly, then the delicious dish will be finished.

B Write down the detailed steps to make your favorite dish according to the sample above.

_____

_____

_____

_____

_____

_____

C Complete the thank-you letter according to the Chinese information.

假设你是韩梅，想写封信给格林先生表示感谢。因为你上周二受格林先生的邀请，到他家参加晚宴。他和家人的热情款待让你度过了一个愉快的夜晚。他家里其乐融融的氛围深深地感染了你。现在你也想邀请格林先生及家人有空来你家做客。

写信日期：2021 年 6 月 9 日

(1)_____

Dear Mr. Green,

I'm writing to express my (2)_____ to you. Last Tuesday, I accepted your kind invitation to have a dinner party at your home. Thanks to the (3)_____ of you and your family, I spent a pleasant evening. The happiness of your family impressed me a lot. Now I would like to (4)_____ to come to my home when you are available.

Please accept my heartfelt thanks and with kindest regards to you and yours.

(5)_____,

Han Mei

Part Four 🏛 Speaking

A Read the following sentence patterns concerning food.

Starter	Response
Do you know how many cuisines there are in China?	Yes, there are eight cuisines in China, which are Sichuan cuisine, Shandong cuisine, Fujian cuisine, Anhui cuisine...

Would you care for / like a drink?	Yes, please. / No, thanks.
What is your favorite food?	My favorite food is...
Can you make a steak?	Of course I can. / No, I have never made it before.
Can you use chopsticks/knife/fork?	No, I'm not used to using...
How would you like your steak done?	Rare/Medium / Medium well / Well done.

B Complete the following dialogue with your own words.

A: Mr. Johnson, please have a seat here. Today you'll have a typical Chinese meal.

B: It all looks wonderful. And I'm so glad to have the chance to try the real thing.

A: Now a toast to the success of our cooperation. Cheers!

B: (1)_____!

A: Mr. Johnson, can you use chopsticks?

B: (2)_____, but I'd like to try.

A: It's easy. In China it's customary to use them this way.

B: Let me try....Oh, it looks easy but it's really difficult.

A: The dishes here are typical of Sichuan cuisine, and they are famous for their particular flavors. This dish is sliced pork in pounded garlic. Please help yourself.

B: Thank you. (3)_____. I really like it.

A: Can I serve you some multi-flavor chicken slices?

B: Thank you. This is delicious too. This food tastes really good.

A: Mr. Johnson, (4)_____. Help yourself to some more crisp duck or anything else you'd like.

B: That tastes delicious, but I can't eat any more.

A: Just a little, please.

B: No more, thanks. (5)_____.

C Introduce a simple dish you're good at making in English.

D Discuss with your partner the differences between Chinese cuisines and Western cuisines.

Project 🗼 Introduce How to Make a Dish

Make a presentation on how to make your favorite dish within 5 minutes using PowerPoint slides, adding some pictures if necessary.

UNIT **6**

Sports

Warm-up

Choose the right option to complete the following dialogue.

> A. What is your favorite sport then?
>
> B. it is good for the metabolism.
>
> C. Are you crazy about sports?
>
> D. I'm too lazy to go out to stretch my legs.
>
> E. You'd better take up some sports.

Paul: (1)_____

Smith: Certainly, I am a super sports fan.

Paul: (2)_____

Smith: Almost all ball games, such as basketball, soccer, volleyball, badminton, table tennis, etc. How about you?

Paul: (3)_____

Smith: (4)_____ Because sports can give you a perfect build and protect you from getting diseases easily.

Paul: Is that so? But sports are tiring sometimes.

King: Actually, (5)_____

Part One 　Listening

Ⓐ Listen to the recording and choose the proper response.

1. A. Yes, please.　　　　　　　B. I'm sorry.
　　C. OK.　　　　　　　　　　D. No, thanks.

2. A. Three years.　　　　　　　B. The whole summer.
　　C. Three hours.　　　　　　　D. Two days.

3. A. Yes, of course.　　　　　　B. It's great.
　　C. Let's go.　　　　　　　　D. It's terrible.

4. A. Two years later.   B. Since I was ten.

C. Since I was born.   D. Since I was grown up.

5. A. Watch TV.   B. Do push-ups.

C. Draw pictures.   D. Play video games.

B Listen to the dialogues and choose the best answer to each question.

1. A. Swimming.   B. Jogging.

C. Playing football.   D. Playing volleyball.

2. A. He doesn't play tennis very well.

B. He is very good at tennis.

C. Nobody can win over him.

D. Nobody loses tennis to him.

3. A. Basketball.   B. Football.

C. Volleyball.   D. All of the above.

4. A. Sports can help him find a mate.

B. He is forced to do it.

C. He is in poor health and needs exercise.

D. Exercise can help him keep fit.

5. A. In the morning.   B. In the afternoon.

C. At noon.   D. In the evening.

C Listen to the following dialogue and fill in the blanks with what you hear.

Mary: What is (1)_____, Li Ming?

Li Ming: A player is offside if he receives a forward pass from a teammate in the opponent's half of the field, with fewer than two (2)_____ between himself and the goal.

Mary: How is a (3)_____ committed?

Li Ming: If a player tricks, (4)_____, (5)_____, obstructs or holds an opponent, he will commit a foul.

Mary: What's the penalty for it?

Li Ming: If it's merely a minor offence, the referee may award a (6)_____. For an intentional offence, the offender may be shown a (7)_____. But if he repeats it intentionally, he may be shown a (8)_____. Then the player is (9)_____ the field.

Mary: Do you think it is a good means to curb violence on the football field?

Li Ming: (10)_____, yes.

Part Two Reading

Text 1

The History of Sports

Sporting activities are **essentially** modified[1] forms of hunting behavior. Viewed **biologically**, the modern footballer is in reality[2] a member of a hunting group. His killing weapon has turned into a harmless football and his prey[3] into a goalmouth. If his aim is accurate and he scores a goal, he enjoys the hunter's triumph[4] of killing his prey.

To understand how this **transformation** has taken place, we must briefly look back at our forefathers. They spent over a million years evolving[5] as cooperative hunters. Their very survival depended on success in the hunting field. Under this pressure, their whole way of life and even their bodies were greatly changed. They became chasers[6], runners, jumpers, aimers, throwers and prey killers. They cooperated as skillful male group **attackers**.

Then about ten thousand years ago, after this immensely[7] long period of hunting for their food, they became farmers. Their improved **intelligence**, so **vital** to their old hunting life, was put to a new use—controlling and **domesticating** their prey. The hunt suddenly became out of date. The food was there on the farms, awaiting[8] their needs. The risks and uncertainties[9] of the hunt were no longer essential for **survival**. The skills and thirst for hunting remained, however, and demanded new outlets[10].

Hunting for sport replaced hunting for **necessity**. This new activity **involved** all the original hunting sequences[11], but the aim of the operation was no longer to avoid **starvation**. Instead the sportsmen set off to test their skills against prey that were no longer essential to their survival. To be sure, the kill may have been eaten, but there were other much simpler ways of obtaining a meaty meal.

In our modern world, sports have become a part of our daily life. People are **crazy** about many kinds of sports. There are two ways to enjoy them, playing or watching them on TV. **Professional** sports are booming[12]. We have pro[13] baseball and soccer. Players are making more money and playing better, and fans are enjoying high-quality games. Some national **athletes** have even gained international attention. Study of the history of sport can teach lessons about social changes and about the nature of sport itself, as sport seems to be involved in the development of **basic** human skill.

---

1. 改良的，改进的 2. 现实，真实 3. 猎物 4. 胜利，成功 5. 进化 6. 追逐者 7. 非常，极大地 8. 等待，等候 9. 不确定性 10. 出口；排放 11. 续发事件 12. 飞速发展，繁荣 13. 职业的，专业的

Vocabulary

essentially	/ɪˈsenʃəli/	*adv.*	本质上；本来
biologically**	/ˌbaɪəˈlɒdʒɪkli/	*adv.*	生物学上，生物学地
transformation**	/ˌtrænsfəˈmeɪʃn/	*n.*	变化，转变
attacker**	/əˈtækə(r)/	*n.*	攻击者，进攻者
intelligence	/ɪnˈtelɪdʒəns/	*n.*	智力，智慧
vital**	/ˈvaɪtl/	*adj.*	极其重要的；必不可少的
domesticate**	/dəˈmestɪkeɪt/	*v.*	驯化
survival	/səˈvaɪvl/	*n.*	幸存，生存
necessity**	/nəˈsesəti/	*n.*	必要，需要
involve*	/ɪnˈvɒlv/	*v.*	包含，涉及
starvation**	/staːˈveɪʃn/	*n.*	饥饿，挨饿
crazy	/ˈkreɪzi/	*adj.*	疯狂的，狂热的
professional**	/prəˈfeʃənl/	*adj.*	职业的，专业的
athlete	/ˈæθliːt/	*n.*	运动员
basic	/ˈbeɪsɪk/	*adj.*	基本的，基础的

Exercises

A Decide whether the following statements are true (T) or false (F) according to the passage.

( ) *1.* The essence of sport is not the hunting behavior.

( ) *2.* Though hunting became obsolete, the skills and desire to hunt remained.

( ) *3.* People's intelligence was important to their old hunting life.

( ) *4.* Hunting for sport replaced hunting for necessity, but the aim of the operation was still to stave off hunger.

( ) *5.* The history of sport involves social changes and the nature of sport itself.

B Fill in each blank with the proper form of the word given in the brackets.

1. The course is _____ (essential) theoretical in orientation.

2. That's what makes the act of rereading so rich and _____ (transform).

3. Sometimes it is _____ (necessarily) to say no.

4. Millions will face _____ (starve) next year as a result of the drought.

5. _____ (athlete) need a good sense of balance.

C Complete the following sentences in English according to the Chinese.

1. 进攻者被击退了。

The _____ was beaten off.

2. 我们的很多行为是由生物机理决定的。

Much of our behavior is _____ determined.

3. 水是生命必不可少的。

Water is a basic _____ of life.

4. 博泰人是第一批驯养马的人。

The Botai were the first to _____ horses.

5. 噪音快把我逼疯了。

That noise is driving me _____.

Text ②

Dragon Dance

One powerful, mythical creature that holds enormous significance in China is the dragon. Think of a Chinese New Year celebration, and you are almost guaranteed to see this, the ancient tradition of dragon dancing. It is especially important at New Year, as the Chinese legend goes, dragons are famed for bringing good luck to any new venture. This traditional art still thrives even in the 21st-century Hong Kong, where the city's skilled dragon dancers are highly sought after. In Kowloon, Andy Kwok leads the Kwok Kung Fu and Dragon Lion Dance Team, one of hundreds across China. We'll come to see the team's final preparations for the festivities.

Dragon dance originated in the Han Dynasty (202 BC–220 AD), which is a collective project. In the process of the dragon dance, we are under the guidance of the dragon ball. With the help of the dragon implements, nine people have finished the whole skillful movements, *you, pan, fan, teng, chuan, chan* and *xi*. Therefore, we should pay more attention to the coordination among team members during the dragon dance training. This is the basic element when completing the dragon dance techniques.

Dragon dance has diversified models and forms. The dragon is a totem of the Chinese nation. The farming tribes worship it very much. People think dragons can make clouds and bring them rain. Playing dragon dances in the spring will hopefully bring people favorable weather; playing in dry seasons will bring them rain; playing to different families will drive ghosts out.

Dragon dance not only exhibits the kind of majestic momentum, but also represents the Chinese vigorous vitality. Dragon dance is not only a physical activity, but also a combination of wisdom and the creation of martial arts, dance, ethnic drums and other sports. Therefore, the custom goes on.

Exercise

Answer the following questions according to the passage.

1. Who leads the Kung Fu and Dragon Lion Dance Team?

_____

2. What is the Chinese legend about dragons?

_____

3. Where did the dragon dance come from?

_____

4. What is the basic element when people complete the techniques of dragon dancing?

_____

5. Why is dragon a totem of the Chinese nation?

_____

Part Three   Writing

A Study the following sample about introducing one's favorite sport.

One of my favorite sports is backcountry hiking, which is going through areas that people seldom visit. However, before I go, I will make sure to have all of the proper gear for the adventure. First of all, I wear clothing and hiking shoes suitable for the current weather conditions. This might include taking water shoes if I have plans for hiking through streams and rivers or a reliable jacket to keep me warm. Next, I will let my family and friends know where I am going and when I will return. Also, I will carry a compass and GPS unit to navigate and locate my position. I will carry a topographical map with me as well. In addition to these items, I will take plenty of food and water, and I will pack a water filter to purify any water I find in streams or lakes. Finally, I will always pack emergency supplies, including a lighter, an emergency blanket, a signaling device like a mirror, and a cellphone. You never know when you will need these things.

B Introduce one of your favorite sports with about 120 words according to the sample in Exercise A.

_____

_____

_____

_____

_____

_____

_____

_____

_____

_____

C Complete the notice of a basketball match according to the Chinese information.

通　　知

本周将有一场激动人心的篮球比赛！

球队：扬州市篮球队 vs. 我校篮球队

地点：篮球场

时间：2021 年 6 月 5 日下午 4 点

主办单位：文娱体育部

请大家穿上运动服去为我校球队加油。如果下雨，比赛将推迟到下周五进行。

文娱体育部

2021 年 6 月 1 日

Notice

There will be (1)_____ this week!

Teams: Yangzhou City basketball team vs. our school basketball team

Venue: (2)_____

Time: 4 p.m., June 5th, 2021

Organizer: (3)_____

(4)_____ should go to cheer on our team in your sportswear.

If it rains, the match will be (5)_____ till next Friday.

Department of Recreation and Sports

June 1st, 2021

Part Four Speaking

A Read the following sentence patterns concerning sports.

Starter	Response
What's your favorite sport?	My favorite sport is…
Do you want to play tennis this afternoon?	Sure, I'd love to!
What kind of activities would you like to take part in?	I'd like to take part in…
Do you often do physical exercises?	Yes, I like sports very much.
Do you want to join in the sports meeting of our school?	Yes, of course.
How often do you go to the gym?	Two or three times a week.
What position do you play?	I'm a goalkeeper.
What's the benefit of doing sports?	It is beneficial to people's physical and mental health.

B Complete the following dialogue with your own words.

Li Ming: Sports are essential in people's life. What kind of sports do you like?

Peter Brown: (1)_____

Li Ming: I also like this kind of sports. It's amazing.

Peter Brown: (2)_____

Li Ming: What is the most popular sport in your country?

Peter Brown: (3)_____

Li Ming: I see. Can you introduce a little bit about your national sport?

Peter Brown: (4)_____

Li Ming: Let me try to play your national game.

Peter Brown: (5)_____

C Talk about one of your favorite sports or sports stars in English.

D Discuss with your partner how to play some popular Chinese ball games, such as volleyball, table tennis, and badminton.

Project Introduce Your Favorite Sport

Introduce your favorite sport within 5 minutes using PowerPoint slides.

UNIT 7

Festival

Warm-up

Choose the right option to complete the following dialogue.

> *A.* Besides, I'm longing for the beautiful beaches there.
>
> *B.* When will you leave?
>
> *C.* This way, please.
>
> *D.* I hope you will have a nice trip.
>
> *E.* Is it always cold at this time in Yangzhou?

Sue: Welcome to our party, Alex.

Alex: Thank you.

Sue: (1)_____

Alex: Thanks. It's so cold today.

Sue: Yeah, it's sunny but cold.

Alex: (2)_____

Sue: Yes, it's usually cold and wet. By the way, what's your plan for the New Year's Day holiday?

Alex: I'm going to Hainan, the weather there is always perfect. (3)_____

Sue: (4)_____

Alex: On December 29. I can't help thinking of it.

Sue: (5)_____

Alex: Thanks. Wow, great party, isn't it?

Sue: Yeah. Everyone seems to be having a good time.

Part One Listening

A **Listen to the recording and choose the proper response.**

1.   A. No, thank you.   B. Yes, of course.

  C. My pleasure.   D. You're right.

2. A. OK, thank you.　　　　　　　B. It doesn't matter.
　 C. It's over there.　　　　　　　D. No way.

3. A. Here you are.　　　　　　　　B. Let's go.
　 C. Why not?　　　　　　　　　　D. Never mind.

4. A. You are so nice.　　　　　　　B. Nice to meet you.
　 C. I'd love to.　　　　　　　　　D. It's great.

5. A. No problem.　　　　　　　　　B. Not at all.
　 C. Is it true?　　　　　　　　　　D. Is it right?

B Listen to the dialogues and choose the best answer to each question.

1. A. The man is not Chinese.
　 B. The man is Chinese.
　 C. The man is used to using chopsticks.
　 D. They are at a coffee bar.

2. A. May Day.　　　　　　　　　　B. Dragon Boat Festival.
　 C. Lantern Festival.　　　　　　　D. Mid-Autumn Day.

3. A. She is asking the man to drink more water.
　 B. She is asking the man to fill in his registration form.
　 C. She is asking the man to help himself to some more beef.
　 D. She is asking the man to have more liquor.

4. A. He will attend the dinner.
　 B. He will watch the firework show.
　 C. He will stay at home.
　 D. He will do nothing.

5. A. He is the host.　　　　　　　　B. He is the guest.
　 C. He is a waiter.　　　　　　　　D. He is the toaster.

C Listen to the following dialogue and fill in the blanks with what you hear.

Da Wei: Li Ming, what's up?

Li Ming: Not much. How about you?

Da Wei: (1) _____. The Spring Festival is coming soon. Is it your

(2) _____ festival?

Li Ming: Yes, it is. It's the most popular and important festival in our country.

Da Wei: The Spring Festival is also my favorite, because I can have a long (3) _____.

Li Ming: What (4) _____ do you usually do for this festival?

Da Wei: We need to clean the house, prepare (5) _____ for family members and buy some (6) _____ food to have a good holiday.

Li Ming: We do the same thing. And how about the Spring Festival (7) _____?

Da Wei: My mum usually makes dumplings. The (8) _____ family have a big dinner together. What about you?

Li Ming: The same as you. We also eat delicious food. After that we watch the Spring Festival Gala and get red (9) _____ from my grandparents.

Da Wei: Interesting. That's our (10) _____.

Part Two Reading

Text 1

The Spring Festival

The first day of the first **lunar** month is the Spring Festival, the beginning of a new year for China. The Spring Festival is China's biggest extravaganza[1] and a day for family **reunion**. Being around family members at the turn of the year is a vital ritual[2] for the Chinese people. Many of those living away from their hometowns return home during the Spring Festival, which gives rise to what's called "the largest **annual** human migration[3] in the world", also known as the "Spring Festival travel rush".

The Spring Festival celebration is a **continuous** process, starting from the 23rd or 24th of the 12th lunar month. People often worship[4] the Kitchen God, clean their houses, do their shopping and put up Spring Festival couplets[5] until New Year's Eve on the lunar **calendar**.

In addition to staying up late on New Year's Eve, having a New Year's Eve dinner and watching the Spring Festival Gala are two important customs of the Spring Festival. The New Year's Eve dinner is manifested[6] in different ways in different parts of China. Those in South China must have a dish of fish, because "fish" in Chinese sounds **similar** to the character for "prosperity"[7] **symbolizing** an abundant[8] and comfortable life. Those in North China often eat dumplings, which symbolize "reunion" and "fortune". The Spring Festival Gala is a **variety** of TV programs broadcast annually to **celebrate** the lunar New Year. The gala attracts the largest audience of any entertainment show in the world, and runs for more than four hours, making it the longest TV show in the world. It is often hailed as a cultural feast for Chinese people on New Year's Eve.

There is also a custom of giving and receiving red envelopes, or *hongbao*. Traditionally, adults placed money into red envelopes and gave them to children to wish them peace and good luck in the coming year. Nowadays, with the **popularization** of mobile **payment** in China, it is a trend to send red envelopes **digitally**. The Internet can **deliver** New Year's wishes to each and every loved one, even if they are thousands of miles away. The joyous **atmosphere** of the Chinese New Year will linger[9] until the first full moon of the first lunar month. Then the Lantern Festival is celebrated, which is bound[10] to be another busy day.

---

1. 盛大表演　2. 仪式；惯例　3. 迁移，移动　4. 祭拜　5. 对联，春联　6. 清楚显示，表明　7. 繁荣
8. 富裕的　9. 缓慢度过；徘徊　10. 一定会，必定的

⛵ Vocabulary

lunar	/ˈluːnə(r)/	*adj.*	阴历的；月球的
reunion	/ˌriːˈjuːniən/	*n.*	团聚，重逢，聚会
annual	/ˈænjuəl/	*adj.*	每年的，年度的
continuous**	/kənˈtɪnjuəs/	*adj.*	连续的，持续的
calendar	/ˈkælɪndə(r)/	*n.*	日历
similar	/ˈsɪmələ(r)/	*adj.*	相似的
symbolize**	/ˈsɪmbəlaɪz/	*v.*	象征；用符号表现
variety**	/vəˈraɪəti/	*n.*	多样；种类
celebrate	/ˈselɪbreɪt/	*v.*	庆祝；过节；祝贺
popularization**	/ˌpɒpjələraɪˈzeɪʃn/	*n.*	普及，大众化
payment**	/ˈpeɪmənt/	*n.*	支付，付款；报酬
digitally	/ˈdɪdʒɪtli/	*adv.*	数码地；数字地
deliver	/dɪˈlɪvə(r)/	*v.*	发表；传递，投递；交付
atmosphere*	/ˈætməsfɪə(r)/	*n.*	气氛；大气

⚓ **Exercises**

Ⓐ **Decide whether the following statements are true (T) or false (F) according to the passage.**

(   ) 1. The first day of the first month is the Spring Festival in China.

(   ) 2. Staying with family members is very important for Chinese people during the Spring Festival.

(   ) 3. Having dinner and watching the Spring Festival Gala on New Year's Day are two important customs.

(   ) 4. In South China, people usually eat dumplings, which means "reunion" and "fortune".

(   ) 5. Nowadays, adults send red envelopes digitally to children through mobile payment.

Ⓑ **Fill in each blank with the proper form of the word given in the brackets.**

1. Two million tourists come _____ (annual) to visit the city.

2. The basic design of the car is very _____ (similar) to that of earlier models.

3. She wanted the _____ (celebrate) to be a simple family affair.

4. It is a good idea to place your order well in advance as _____ (deliver) can often take months rather than weeks.

5. Make sure that you don't have to _____ (payment) expensive excess charges.

Ⓒ **Complete the following sentences in English according to the Chinese.**

1. 除了基本工资外，还有一系列额外福利。

_____ basic salary, there's a list of extra benefits.

2. 奥运五环象征着五大洲。

The five Olympic rings _____ five continents.

3. 从早上到现在雨就没有停过。

The rain has been _____ since this morning.

4. 所供应的菜肴之丰盛让我心动。

I was impressed by the _____ of dishes on offer.

5. 私家车的普及有很多好处。

The _____ of private cars has many advantages.

Text ②

Qixi Festival

The seventh day of the seventh lunar month is Qixi, widely regarded as China's Valentine's Day.

Many different stories lay claim to being the origin of the festival, but one version is the most popular and accepted. The youngest daughter of the Jade Emperor (the ruler of the world in legend), the Weaver Girl was a fairy who weaved rosy clouds in the sky. She became tired of the boring immortal life and decided to descend to the mortal world. She met and fell in love with a cowherd. The Jade Emperor strongly objected to the couple's union and forcibly separated them by the Milky Way leaving them torn apart by the galaxy and only allowing them to meet once a year. Despite that, the distance could not stop their love for each other. They still love each other and look forward to meeting once a year on the seventh day of the seventh lunar month.

On the brighter side, the tragedy of the Cowherd and the Weaver Girl could not happen in modern China. With the development of high-speed railways, lovebirds no longer have any difficulty reuniting even if they are many miles apart. Beijing and Shanghai, the two largest cities in China, are 1,200 kilometers away from each other. But a ride on the high-speed rail only takes four hours and there are more than 100 high-speed trains travelling between the two cities every day. The convenience and efficiency of modern travel have shortened the "galactic distance" between couples.

More than 2,000 years ago, Qixi was also known as "the Begging Festival". In ancient China, women would visit their close friends and worship the Weaver Girl on the seventh day of the seventh lunar month praying they could become as clever as the Weaver Girl and find their faithful lover. In traditional Chinese marriage, women who pray for dexterity often devote all their energies to family life. However, times have changed as has the role of women. A more diversified social role enables women in China to pursue their love courageously and no longer be bound to domestic life like the Weaver Girl.

High-speed rail has brought tremendous changes. Many Chinese traditions have changed, but the tradition of festive reunions has stayed strong.

Exercise

Answer the following questions according to the passage.

1. When is Qixi Festival?
   _____

2. Who is the Weaver Girl?
   _____

3. How did the Jade Emperor punish the Weaver Girl and the Cowherd?
   _____

4. How long does it take from Beijing to Shanghai by high-speed train?
   _____

5. Why did women worship the Weaver Girl in ancient China?
   _____

Part Three Writing

A Study the following sample about introducing a festival.

The Qingming Festival, also known as Tomb-sweeping Day, is a traditional Chinese festival observed from the Han Dynasty. It falls on the first day of the fifth solar term of the Chinese lunar calendar. This makes it the 15th day after the Spring Equinox, i.e. April 4th or 5th in a given year.

During Qingming Festival, Chinese families visit the tombs of their ancestors to clean the gravesites, pray to their ancestors, and make ritual offerings. This holiday is associated with the consumption of *qingtuan*, or green dumplings made of glutinous rice and mugwort.

B Introduce one of the Chinese festivals briefly, including its specific date, customs, etc.

_____

_____

_____

_____

_____

_____

_____

_____

_____

_____

C Complete the invitation letter according to the Chinese information.

亲爱的布莱克：

新的一年即将来临，学生会准备举办一场元旦晚会。聚会时间是 12 月 29 日星期五晚上 6：00 至 7：30，地点在学校俱乐部。我很高兴邀请你来参加。我们还邀请了另外两位外教 Frazer 和 Gree。请加入我们一起庆祝新年。希望你能 5：50 到场。期待能在那天见到你。

李明

2021 年 12 月 15 日

(1)_____

Dear Blake,

    (2)_____. The Student Union will hold a party to celebrate it. The party will take place (3)_____ from 6:00 p.m. to 7:30 p.m. on Friday, December 29th, 2021. I'm pleased to invite you to the party. Another two foreign teachers, Mr. Frazer and Miss Gree (4)_____. Please join us. You are hoped to arrive at 5:50 p.m. (5)_____.

                                                        Sincerely yours,

                                                        Li Ming

Part Four Speaking

A Read the following sentence patterns concerning festivals.

Starter	Response
Happy holidays! Merry Christmas / Happy New Year!	Thanks, you too. Merry Christmas / Happy New Year!
What festival is it today?	It's...
I'm hosting a New Year party. Do you want to come?	Sounds awesome, I'll be there. Sorry, I'm going to another one.
What is your favorite festival?	My favorite festival is...
Why do you like the Spring Festival?	Because the whole family can get together and...
What do you usually do during the Dragon Boat Festival?	We usually enjoy the dragon boat racing and eat *Zongzi*.
How was your Spring Festival?	I've had a good time with my family.

B Complete the following dialogue with your own words.

    A: Hi! Long time no see. Let's go and have a drink.

    B: (1)_____

    A: What's your favorite festival?

    B: (2)_____

    A: What do you do in this festival?

    B: (3)_____

    A: Is there any traditional food?

    B: (4)_____ What about you? Which
        is your favorite festival?

    A: (5)_____

    B: Why?

    A: (6)_____

    B: It sounds wonderful.

C Talk about your favorite festival with your classmates, including its specific date, origin, customs, etc.

D Discuss with your partner the differences between Chinese festivals and Western festivals.

Project   Tell a Story Related to Chinese Festivals

Work in groups to find more information about traditional Chinese festivals and tell a story related to one of them in detail using PowerPoint slides.

UNIT **8**

Money

Warm-up

Choose the right option to complete the following dialogue.

> A. How about a savings account?
>
> B. I'd like to open an account.
>
> C. 3-year term and 12,000 dollars.
>
> D. How much do you plan to deposit?
>
> E. Please fill out this form.

Clerk: Good morning, sir. Can I help you?

John: Yes. (1)_____

Clerk: What kind of account do you want?

John: A current account, please.

Clerk: (2)_____

John: OK! What's your interest rate for current accounts?

Clerk: 1.5% per year at present.

John: (3)_____

Clerk: It is 3.5% per year.

John: OK! I want to have a 3-year term savings account.

Clerk: No problem, sir. (4)_____

John: $12,000.

Clerk: (5)_____

John: Yes, thank you very much.

Part One Listening

A Listen to the recording and choose the proper response.

1. A. Quite a lot.   B. My pleasure.

    C. Thank you very much.   D. Yes, but he's not in.

2. A. Wait a minute.   B. Yes, I do.

   C. See you later.   D. Fine, thanks.

3. A. Take it easy.   B. Mind your step.

   C. Very much.   D. So am I.

4. A. At 16:30.   B. No, thanks.

   C. Here we are.   D. Can I help you?

5. A. This way, please.   B. Sure. Here it is.

   C. It's far away.   D. Take care.

B **Listen to the dialogues and choose the best answer to each question.**

1. A. Change some money.   B. Buy some traveler's checks.

   C. Deposit some money.   D. Exchange some money.

2. A. It's closed.   B. 12:00 noon to 9 p.m.

   C. 9 a.m. to 5 p.m.   D. 9 a.m. to 12:00 noon.

3. A. Open an account.   B. Withdraw some money.

   C. Deposit some money.   D. Exchange some money.

4. A. Withdraw some money.   B. Apply for a credit card.

   C. Wire some money.   D. Exchange some money.

5. A. Where to change some money.   B. What the service charge is.

   C. How to buy traveler's checks.   D. Where to buy traveler's checks.

C **Listen to the following dialogue and fill in the blanks with what you hear.**

Peter: Hey, how are you?

Nancy: Just the (1)_____. How about you?

Peter: Everything is OK. Oh, my God! You are reading *The Secret of Managing Your Money*!

Nancy: Yes! You can't (2)_____ you are talking to a billionaire-to-be.

Peter: OK! OK! I can see you are very (3)_____ about money now. You are greedy!

Nancy: Not the case. I have to start living on a (4)_____, or I can never live a good life.

Peter: No, you are wrong. Money can't buy (5)_____.

Nancy: I see. But an (6)_____ goes: "Money talks." Money is not everything, but we can buy nothing without money.

Peter: Remember that money is important, but it is not the most important thing. Without love, (7)_____ or health, money is nothing.

Nancy: Yes, but I'm often (8)_____ and I'm flat broke right now. To stay (9)_____ a budget is of great help for me now.

Peter: Maybe you are right. But health comes first! Let's go to dinner. I have invited Judy.

Nancy: Judy? The girl with big eyes and long hair, working in ICBC?

Peter: Yes! You know she is a (10)_____ and she works as a financial consultant there. You can ask her for some advice.

Nancy: Good idea! I can't wait to see her.

Part Three 🛥 Reading

Text 1

Making Something from Nothing

What would you do to make money if all you had was five dollars and two hours? This is the **assignment** I gave students in one of my classes at Stanford University. Most of my students **seriously** took the challenge and **exposed** a wealth of possibilities[1].

So what did they do? All of the teams were remarkably[2] **inventive**. One group noticed a problem common in a lot of college towns—the long lines at popular restaurants on Saturday nights. The team decided to help those people who didn't want to wait in line. They booked **reservations** at several restaurants. As the time for their reservations **approached**, they sold each reservation for up to 20 dollars to customers who were happy to **avoid** a long wait.

Another team took an even simpler approach. They set up a stand in front of the Student Union where they offered to **measure** bicycle tire[3] pressure[4] for free. If the tires needed filling, they added air for one dollar. After their first few customers, the students found that the bicyclists were incredibly[5] grateful. They realized that they were providing a **convenient** and valuable service. In fact, halfway through the two-hour period, the team stopped asking for a **specific** payment and requested **donations** instead. Their income soared[6]. Their customers paid more for a free service than when asked to pay a fixed price.

Each of these projects brought in a few hundred dollars. However, the winning team looked at the task in a **totally** different way and made $650. These students **determined** that the most valuable resource was neither the five dollars nor the two hours but their three-minute presentation time on Monday. They decided to sell it to a company that wanted to recruit[7] the students in the class. The team created a three-minute "commercial" for that company and showed it in their presentation. This was brilliant[8].

The exercises described above highlight several points. First, opportunities are abundant. At any place and time you can look around and **identify** problems that need solving. Second, regardless of the size of the problem, there are usually **creative** ways to use the resources already in your hands to solve them. Third, we so often frame[9] problems too tightly. People who participated in these projects took this lesson to heart. Many reflected afterward that they would never have an excuse for being broke, since there is always a nearby fortune begging to be won.

---

1. 可能性　2. 惊人地；显著地　3. 轮胎　4. 压力　5. 非常地；难以置信地　6. 激增　7. 招聘　8. 绝妙的；成功的　9. 设计；制订，拟订

Vocabulary

assignment**	/ə'saɪnmənt/	*n.*	作业；任务
seriously	/'sɪəriəsli/	*adv.*	认真地；严肃地
expose*	/ek'spəuz/	*v.*	显示；揭露
inventive**	/ɪn'ventɪv/	*adj.*	有创造力的
reservation**	/ˌrezə'veɪʃn/	*n.*	预订，保留
approach	/ə'prəutʃ/	*v./n.*	临近，接近；方式，方法
avoid	/ə'vɔɪd/	*v.*	避免
measure	/'meʒə(r)/	*v.*	测量
convenient	/kən'viːniənt/	*adj.*	方便的
specific	/spə'sɪfɪk/	*adj.*	特定的，特殊的
donation	/dəu'neɪʃn/	*n.*	捐款
totally	/'təutəli/	*adv.*	完全地

determine	/dɪˈtɜːmɪn/	v.	判定；确定；作出决定，下决心
identify*	/aɪˈdentɪfaɪ/	v.	辨别；确定
creative	/kriˈeɪtɪv/	adj.	创造性的

Exercises

A Decide whether the following statements are true (T) or false (F) according to the passage.

(   ) 1. One group of students found there was a long queue at popular restaurants on Sunday nights.

(   ) 2. Students sold reservations to customers who didn't want to wait.

(   ) 3. Another group set up a stand to measure bicycle tire pressure and charged for one dollar.

(   ) 4. The winning team made a three-minute advertising for a company.

(   ) 5. We should use the resources in our hands to solve problems creatively.

B Fill in each blank with the proper form of the word given in the brackets.

1. The teacher _____ (assignment) a different task to each of the children.

2. He seemed to have predicted numbers of _____ (inventive) that only came about hundreds of years later, like flying machines and so on.

3. The money from the tour can be _____ (donation) to help people in need.

4. It is only our _____ (determine) to fight that has pulled us through.

5. Many people are enthusiastic about online shopping because of its _____ (convenient).

C Complete the following sentences in English according to the Chinese.

1. 他看见她玩这个游戏十分认真的样子，觉得好笑。
   He was amused to see how _____ she took the game.

2. 我要给饭店打个电话预订座位。
   I'll call the restaurant and make a _____.

3. 他们避免黄昏后独自出门。

They _____ going out alone after dark.

4. 乘客需要先确认自己的旅行箱再上飞机。

Passengers were asked to _____ their own suitcases before boarding the plane.

5. 他不想向任何人显露自己的恐惧与不安。

He did not want to _____ his fears and insecurity to anyone.

Text ②

The History of Money

Money has got a very colorful history because a number of things have been used in the place of what we use as money, like feathers, shells, cloth…In Roman times the Roman soldiers were paid in salt and that is how we get the word *salary*, from the Latin word *sal* for *salt*.

And a number of tribes used cattle which were useful because they were transportable. But they were quite bulky and you weren't always sure of the size of cattle you were going to get, so there was a problem there of quality.

In the 7th century, we had money in the form of precious metal. There was always a problem of making sure that the coin that you got had enough precious metal in it to give it a value. When things got tough, you often found some civilizations were quite good at what they called sweating the money, which was effectively taking out the precious metal content so that what you got actually wasn't what you thought you got. In those days, Spanish coins were used a lot. Sometimes, stores used certain tokens because there is a shortage of actual coinage. And then, there is money as we know today in notes and coins.

In the 9th century in China, we had paper money for the first time. It wasn't quite the paper money that we know today. It was more like a piece of paper saying a promise to pay.

Throughout the history there are three functions of money. Firstly, it's a medium of exchange, so it's some commodity that facilitates the exchange of goods and services. Secondly, it is a unit of account, which means that we use money to reckon prices and values for comparisons between goods and services or over time. Thirdly, money is a store of value. It is an asset. It's something that we can use to store value away to be retrieved at a later point in time. That is to say, we can hold money and transfer the consumption power to some point in the future.

⚓ Exercise

Answer the following questions according to the passage.

1. What did soldiers get as salary in Roman times?

_____

2. What were the problems when people exchanged with cattle in some tribes?

_____

3. What was the problem when people used precious metal as money?

_____

4. When and where did the paper money first appear?

_____

5. What are the functions of money?

_____

Part Three 🗼 Writing

A Study the following sample to learn how to describe a picture.

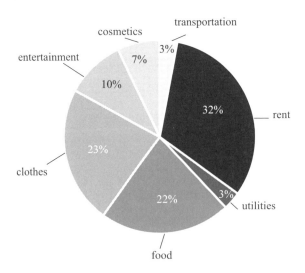

Monthly expenses of a female office worker

This chart shows the monthly expenses of a female office worker. It is divided into several categories, like rent, clothes, food, entertainment and so on.

It's clear that rent accounts for the most of a female office worker's expenses. Clothes and food account for almost a quarter respectively. Only 3 percent each is spent on transportation and utilities. The chart illustrates that a female office worker spends a little more on cosmetics and entertainment, which make up 7 percent and 10 percent respectively.

Of the expenses shown in the pie chart, it does seem that a female office worker spends a little too much on clothes. It might be better if some of this money could be put aside as savings.

To sum up, a female office worker's expenses seem reasonable, but her monthly wage could be used more effectively.

B Describe the picture and express your views on saving money with about 120 words.

"To save or not to save?"

_____

_____

_____

_____

_____

_____

_____

_____

_____

C Complete the E-mail according to the Chinese information.

发件人：李明   收件人：Chris

发件人电子邮箱：liming@126.com   收件人电子邮箱：Chris@126.com

内容：

• 告知对方你已于昨天按期收到第一批 50 台型号为 X10 的电脑；

• 经过检查，发现其中一台在运输过程中由于包装原因被损坏；

• 希望对方能补发一台同样型号的电脑，或退还一台电脑的货款。

To: (1)_____

From: (2)_____

Subject: About the first batch of computers

Date: May 21, 2021

Dear Chris,

    We received the first 50 computers of model X10 (3)_____ yesterday. After inspection, (4)_____ due to packing during transportation. I hope you can deliver a new set of computer with (5)_____, or give us a refund.

Yours,

Li Ming

Part Four Speaking

A Read the following sentence patterns concerning money.

Starter	Response
What kind of account would you like to open?	Checking/Savings/Current account.
How much money would you like to deposit/withdraw?	I'd like to deposit/withdraw $500.
Could you tell me the exchange rate for U.S. dollars today?	It's 671.32 RMB for 100 USD.
May I know the interest rate?	It's 1.2%.
How would you like to pay for your purchase, cash or card?	I'd like to pay by card / in cash.
I need to transfer funds to a different account, please.	Please fill out this form.

B Complete the following dialogue with your own words.

A: Good morning. What can I do for you?

B: (1)_____

A: A current account or a savings account?

B: (2)_____

A: OK. Please fill out this form and show your ID card.

B: (3)_____

A: How much do you want to deposit?

B: (4)_____

A: It varies from time to time. At present it is 0.9%.

B: (5)_____

C Talk about different currencies in the world with your partner and make a dialogue about exchanging money.

D Which is your motto, "A penny saved is a penny earned" or "Money makes the world go around"? Discuss with your partner and give your opinion.

Project　Make a Money Management Plan

Work in groups to draw a chart of your monthly money management plan and give a presentation before the class.

UNIT 9

Travel

Warm-up

Choose the right option to complete the following dialogue.

> A. That sounds perfect!
>
> B. we can take photos of Dunhuang.
>
> C. So far so good.
>
> D. Do you have any plans?
>
> E. Shall we leave in five days?

Steve: Hey, Mary! How is everything going?

Mary: (1)_____ Thank you. How about you?

Steve: Pretty well. Mary, have you heard we've got two weeks off this summer?

Mary: Yeah, sure. (2)_____

Steve: How about going to Dunhuang for a holiday?

Mary: (3)_____ It's the place I have always wanted to go.

Steve: I'll book the air tickets right away. (4)_____

Mary: In five days? How marvelous! We'd better take a camera with us so that (5)_____

Steve: That's a good idea. We can also take a camel ride on Mingsha Mountain.

Mary: Wow, it must be very interesting. I can't wait for that! See you then.

Steve: See you!

Part One Listening

A Listen to the recording and choose the proper response.

1. A. No way.   B. It's over there.

   C. It doesn't matter.   D. OK, thank you.

2. A. Not at all.   B. Let's go.

   C. Never mind.   D. Here you are.

3. A. It's great.   B. I'd love to.

C. You're so nice.   D. Don't worry.

4. A. Good idea.   B. No, thanks.

C. Yes, very much.   D. That's all right.

5. A. Yes, once a month.   B. By train.

C. See you again.   D. It doesn't matter.

B **Listen to the dialogues and choose the best answer to each question.**

1. A. At an airport.   B. At a hotel.

C. At a travel agency.   D. In Paris.

2. A. At a restaurant.   B. In a coffee shop.

C. In a dining room.   D. On a plane.

3. A. At his office.   B. Out for lunch.

C. At a travel agency.   D. At a bakery.

4. A. What the flight number is.   B. Where to find a telephone.

C. What time the flight departs. D. Where to board the plane.

5. A. Spain.   B. Canada.

C. Europe.   D. Australia.

C **Listen to the following dialogue and fill in the blanks with what you hear.**

Airport staff: Good morning, what can I do for you?

Passenger: Yes, I'd like to check in for the (1)_____ to Sydney, please.

Airport staff: May I see your (2)_____ and ticket, please?

Passenger: Sure, here you are.

Airport staff: Thank you, madam. What type of (3)_____ do you prefer?

Passenger: May I have an aisle seat?

Airport staff: Aisle seat? (4)_____. Do you have any luggage to (5)_____?

Passenger: Yes, I have one bag to check in and a bag to (6)_____. What's the luggage (7)_____?

Airport staff: Well, 15 kilos per passenger. Your bag is only 7 kilos.

Passenger: Thank you.

Airport staff: Here is your boarding pass, madam. The flight will begin (8)_____ at 4:30 p.m. at Gate (9)_____.

Passenger: Thank you very much.

Airport staff: Have a (10)_____ flight.

Part Two　Reading

Text 1

Travel Slows Down

We all want to go somewhere—somewhere that has been on our bucket list[1] for ages. So, when the chance arises, we tend to squeeze[2] as many **sights** into the trip as we can—four cities in seven days, "must-see's" in Tokyo, famous **landmarks** in Europe. It's as if the faster we're checking things off our list, the more we are experiencing.

However, when it comes to travel, it's probably not quantity that counts but quality. *Traveler*, the South Korean reality show, can perhaps give us some idea of what travel is like at its best.

Like many travel-themed[3] shows, *Traveler*, which debuted on Feb. 21, **features** two celebrities[4]—Ryu Jun-yeol, 33, and Lee Je-hoon, 35. But unlike other cookie-cutter[5] travel shows, *Traveler*'s travelers don't have a mission and there isn't a competition for them to win. Instead, it focuses on "depicting[6] the real **experience** of traveling by showing the processes of finding a place to stay or grabbing a taxi", according to *The Korea Times*. In other words, Ryu and Lee are given total freedom to **explore**, for example, Cuba, the Central American country, without any interference[7]—or help—from a production team.

This is actually the philosophy of what's called "slow travel", which is **trending** among the world's more **adventurous** journeyers[8].

Slow travel isn't about getting somewhere as quickly as possible, but about simply being excited as you're getting there, or not getting there at all.

You may try to **wander** off the main road and take a back street instead. You may **ignore** the guidebook's **recommendation** and ask **local** people where they prefer to eat and hang out[9]. And you'll be surprised by what a place has to offer when you're not busy **rushing** around and checking things off your bucket list.

"Travel is just like life," said Ryu in the show. "There is little fun in it if everything is **predictable**."

It's true that we all want to go "somewhere". But as travel **blog** CheeseWeb puts it, as long as you keep an open mind, you'll see that "everywhere is 'somewhere'."

---

1. 人生愿望清单　2. 挤进；塞满　3. 以旅行为主题的　4. 名人，知名人士　5. 千篇一律的　6. 描绘，描述
7. 干涉，干扰　8. 旅行者　9. 闲逛

⛵ **Vocabulary**

sight	/saɪt/	*n.*	名胜，风景
landmark**	/ˈlændmɑːk/	*n.*	地标
feature	/ˈfiːtʃə(r)/	*v.*	由……主演
experience	/ɪkˈspɪəriəns/	*n.*	（一次）经历，体验
explore	/ɪkˈsplɔː(r)/	*v.*	探索，探险
trend*	/trend/	*v.*	有……的趋势，趋向
adventurous**	/ədˈventʃərəs/	*adj.*	有冒险精神的
wander*	/ˈwɒndə(r)/	*v.*	（指人或动物）离开原处或正道
ignore	/ɪɡˈnɔː(r)/	*v.*	忽视；对……不予理会
recommendation	/ˌrekəmenˈdeɪʃn/	*n.*	推荐；介绍
local	/ˈləʊkl/	*adj.*	当地的，本地的
rush	/rʌʃ/	*v.*	迅速移动；急着（做）
predictable**	/prɪˈdɪktəbl/	*adj.*	可预见的，可预料的
blog**	/blɒɡ/	*n.*	博客

Exercises

A Decide whether the following statements are true (T) or false (F) according to the passage.

(   ) **1.** *Traveler*, like other travel shows, focused on competitions or missions performed by celebrities to attract audiences.

(   ) **2.** "Slow travel" is the current trend which is popular among the more adventurous journeyers worldwide.

(   ) **3.** People taking slow travel want to get somewhere as quickly as possible.

(   ) **4.** If you ignore the guidebook's recommendation while traveling, you'll lose a lot of fun.

(   ) **5.** As Ryu said, "There is little fun in travel if everything is predictable."

B Fill in each blank with the proper form of the word given in the brackets.

1. What is your _____ (recommend) concerning this issue?

2. She saw a stranger _____ (wander) in the garden.

3. Tibet is a favorite destination among more _____ (adventure) travelers.

4. Those brave _____ (explore) reached the South Pole.

5. No matter you are a lion or a deer, you have _____ (rush) yourself off your feet for living.

C Complete the following sentences in English according to the Chinese.

1. 他推荐的餐厅与我们心目中的相去甚远。

The restaurant he _____ fell far short of our expectation.

2. 经验与理论有相同的价值。

_____ is equally as valuable as theory.

3. 他总是严于律人，宽于待己。

He always _____ his faults and criticizes others.

4. 当地的店主向旅游者出售纪念品。

The _____ shopkeepers sell souvenirs to tourists.

5. 那日出真是一幅美景。

The sunrise was a very beautiful _____.

Text 2

Best Places to Visit in China

China, the gateway to East Asia, is a fascinating country. Visitors making their first trip to China usually stick to the larger cities. More experienced visitors to China will strike out in other directions. We're traveling maybe a bit more frustrating because of the language barrier, but most definitely doable for independent travelers.

Here's a list of the best places to visit in China.

Number 6: Jiuzhaigou

Jiuzhaigou Valley has been described as a fairyland, because of its many waterfalls, snow-covered karst mountains, and its 108 blue turquoise and green colored lakes that are so crystal clear that one can see the bottoms.

Number 5: Hangzhou

Famed for its natural scenery, Hangzhou and its West Lake have been immortalized by countless poets and artists. In the 13th century, Marco Polo described the city as the most beautiful and magnificent in the world.

Number 4: Yangshuo

Yangshuo, in South China, was once a magnet for backpackers, because of its cheap prices and laid-back atmosphere. But today it draws all sorts of travelers to enjoy its beautiful scenery and karst mountains. Yangshuo also makes a good base to take a day trip to Guilin, for a leisurely trip on the Li River.

Number 3: Xi'an

Xi'an was once the start of the indispensable Silk Road, which made commerce between many countries in Eurasia possible. It was also the imperial seat for no fewer than eleven dynasties between 1,000 BC and 1,000 AD. Its most famous attraction is the Terracotta Army, the protectors of the tomb of the first emperor of China.

Number 2: Shanghai

Shanghai is the largest city in China. Its skyline is filled with skyscrapers while shiny shopping malls, luxurious hotels, and prestigious art centers are rising alongside. The city nights in Shanghai are representative of the beautiful view of China cities, with bright neon signs, bustling streets and numerous businesses. The most popular place to go for a stroll is the Bund, Shanghai's riverfront along the Huangpu River.

Number 1: Beijing

Beijing is the capital city and remains one of the most popular places to visit in China. Its history dates back to more than 3,000 years ago and much of that history is still alive within its borders. The city is home to Tian'anmen Square, the Forbidden City, the National Museum of China, the Summer Palace, as well as the Great Wall. These and other attractions are perfect for observing Chinese gardens, ancient architecture and Chinese culture from a range of periods in the country's long history.

Exercise

Answer the following questions according to the passage.

1. Why has Jiuzhaigou been depicted as a wonderland?

2. Which city in China was the start of the Silk Road?

3. Where is the most popular place for foreigners to take around in Shanghai?

4. What are the famous scenic spots in Beijing?

5. Where do you want to go? Why?

Part Three 🛑 Writing

A Study the following sample about introducing a tourist attraction.

Yangzhou is located in the center of Jiangsu Province, and the Grand Canal passes through the city. It is a typical consumer city, with a developed economy and culture.

Yangzhou is among the 24 historical and cultural cities, which were made public by the state. In the Sui Dynasty, Yangzhou became a southeast metropolis due to the construction of the Grand Canal which gave facilities for the transportation of salt by water. In the Tang Dynasty, Yangzhou was the largest business and foreign trade center in China and saw its prosperity never known before.

Yangzhou, with its picturesque scenery, is a tourist city well known. The classic garden of Yangzhou is distinctive and turns out to be one of the favorites of tourists from China and abroad.

B Introduce one of your dream cities with about 120 words, including the location, scenic spots, culture, etc.

_____

_____

_____

_____

_____

_____

_____

_____

_____

_____

C Complete the customer feedback table according to the Chinese information.

顾客姓名：张建林

顾客邮箱：zhanggj1999@163.com

内容：酒店员工非常友好，提供了良好的服务。酒店的房间干净整洁，餐厅的食物美味可口，住店的体验很不错。但是酒店离市中心较远，建议增设从酒店到地铁站的班车，为客人提供方便。

Customer Feedback Table

Name: Zhang Jianlin

Email address: Zhanggj1999@163.com

Comments:

The staff are kind and provide me (1)_____. It's a great experience for me to stay in (2)_____ and I also (3)_____ in the dining hall. However, for the convenience of the guests, I (4)_____ can be arranged between the hotel and the subway station because (5)_____.

Part Four 🗼 Speaking

A Read the following sentence patterns concerning travel.

Starter	Response
Have you been here before?	No, it is my first visit to...
How about going to...for holidays?	That's wonderful.
Could you take me around the city?	Yes, of course. There are a lot of scenic spots here.
Do you know the history of this city?	Certainly. Its history can date back to more than...years ago.
What's your impression on the city?	I was deeply impressed by...
Do you have any luggage to check in?	Yes, I have one suitcase to check in and one bag to carry on.
What type of seat do you prefer, window or aisle?	Aisle, please.

B Complete the following dialogue with your own words.

Reservationist: Good morning, Paradise Hotel. What can I do for you?

Guest: (1)_____

Reservationist: OK, sir. For which date?

Guest: (2)_____

Reservationist: What kind of room would you like, a double or a single?

Guest: (3)_____

Reservationist: OK, may I have your name, please?

Guest: (4)_____

Reservationist: Could you give me a contact number, please?

Guest: (5)_____

Reservationist: Alright, thank you very much. We look forward to seeing you then.

C What certificates are essential when traveling abroad? Can you make a list of them?

D Discuss with your partner some Do's and Don'ts when traveling abroad.

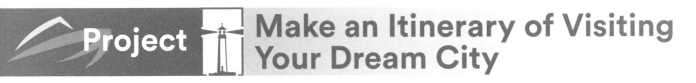

Project 🗼 Make an Itinerary of Visiting Your Dream City

Make a 5-day itinerary of visiting your dream city.

Day	Destination	Scenic Spots	Accommodation	Transportation

UNIT 10
Entertainment

Warm-up

Choose the right option to complete the following dialogue.

> A. What kind of movie do you like?
>
> B. Yeah, I could hardly wait to see it.
>
> C. you like all movies except the horror ones.
>
> D. Is it a horror movie?
>
> E. Would you like to go with me next weekend?

Gary: I've heard *The Saw* would be on next week. I want to see it.

May: (1)_____

Gary: Yeah, I love horror movies the most. (2)_____

May: No way. I will be scared out of my wits.

Gary: Well. (3)_____

May: Let me see. Romance, comedy, action, science fiction, cartoon, and so on.

Gary: In a word, (4)_____

May: Yeah, it seems like we don't talk the same language when it comes to movie.

Gary: Not quite. I also like romance and comedy movies very much.

May: *The Terminal* is a movie of this type.

Gary: So, we can relax now.

May: (5)_____

Part One Listening

Ⓐ Listen to the recording and choose the proper response.

1. A. You are late.　　　　　　　　B. Don't mention it.

　　C. Go ahead, please.　　　　　D. OK.

2. A. Thank you.   B. Sure.

    C. Not too bad.   D. It's over there.

3. A. Not at all.   B. That's all right.

    C. No, I didn't.   D. Don't worry.

4. A. It doesn't matter.   B. Not at all.

    C. I didn't think so.   D. Very good.

5. A. Yes, I am.   B. Thank you for coming.

    C. It's too late.   D. Here you are.

B **Listen to the dialogues and choose the best answer to each question.**

1. A. She should move to another place.

    B. The neighbors probably won't turn down the music.

    C. He wants to listen to different music.

    D. He doesn't think the music is particularly loud.

2. A. She played the piano.   B. She went to a concert.

    C. She wrote some letters.   D. She practiced singing.

3. A. Five dollars   B. Two dollars.

    C. Nine dollars.   D. Four dollars.

4. A. She doesn't like music.

    B. She likes to play musical instruments.

    C. She's fond of listening to music.

    D. She likes to listen to records and play instruments.

5. A. She likes classical music.   B. She needs 100 records.

    C. She plays jazz music.   D. She is a jazz fan.

C **Listen to the following monologue and fill in the blanks with what you hear.**

I really enjoy listening to music because it helps me (1)_____ and takes my (2)_____ away from other cares of the day.

Personally, I like jazz music because of its (3)_____ rhythms and soothing beats. There are (4)_____ stations on the radio that play this type of music. Other times, I enjoy listening to (5)_____ and western music. Some of the lyrics to these songs are inspirational and (6)_____. Occasionally, I listen to classic rock or classical music, but I can't stand heavy metal or rap music.

When I'm on the road, I either (7)_____ my radio to a favorite station, or I listen to music on my MP3 player. I've (8)_____ hundreds of songs to my player, so it's easy to (9)_____ and play my favorite music. When I get home, I (10)_____ my stereo system, crank up the volume, and enjoy the music.

Part Two Reading

Text 1

Journey to the West

Journey to the West is one of the Four Great Classical Novels of Chinese literature, written by Wu Cheng'en, a novelist and poet of the Ming Dynasty (1368—1644). The novel is based on the actual 7th-century pilgrimage[1] of the Tang monk[2] Xuanzang (602—664) to the Western Paradise in search of the true scriptures[3]. The story itself was already a part of Chinese **folk** and literary tradition in the form of colloquial stories when Wu Cheng'en formed it into his long and richly **humorous** novel.

Composed of 100 chapters, this fantasy can be divided into three major sections. The first seven chapters recount the birth of the Monkey King and his rebellion[4] against the Heaven, and its **acquisition** of magic powers. The following Five chapters relate the story of Xuanzang, and why he is searching for the scriptures, as well as his preparations for the journey. The rest of the story **recounts** the entertaining story of Xuanzang and his three disciples, Sun Wukong (Monkey), Zhu Bajie (Pig) and Sha Wujing (Friar Sand), who set out on an **arduous** journey to the West, involving 81 adventures. Along their journey, they help the local inhabitants by defeating various monsters and demons who try to obtain immortality by eating Xuanzang's flesh. And after overcoming many dangers, they finally arrive at the destination and then culminates[5] in their **attainment** of the true scriptures.

The leading role, Sun Wukong, who has great magical powers, is a **righteous** and brave hero who has mastered 72 methods of transformation. Unlike conventional heroes, he departs from tradition and fights for freedom. His tag is, "Hey, I'm coming!" Wukong uses his talents to fight demons and play pranks[6]. However, his behavior is checked by a headband placed around his head by Guanyin to force him to be good. The headband causes Wukong unbearable headaches when Xuanzang **recites** the Tight Headband spell[7] (taught to him by Guanyin) whenever he needs to chastise him.

Wukong's child-like playfulness is a huge contrast to his **cunning** mind. This, coupled with his great power, makes him a **likeable** hero, though not necessarily a good role model. His antics[8] present a lighter side during the long and dangerous trip into the unknown. He defeated powerful demons on the pilgrimage and helped Xuanzang accomplish his objective with Bajie and monk Wujing.

As one of the most popular Chinese folk novels, *Journey to the West* is notable for its multiple rhetorical[9] styles that reflect the dialects and **regional** cultural idiosyncrasies[10] that Xuanzang and the Monkey encounter on their journey. The novel is enjoyed for its biting satire[11] of society and for its allegorical[12] presentation of human striving and **perseverance**. *Journey to the West* tells stories about self-discipline and overcoming difficulties. It has a **profound** influence on the Chinese spirit.

---

1. 朝圣　2. 僧人　3. 真经　4. 反抗　5. 结束，告终　6. 恶作剧　7. 紧箍咒　8. 滑稽的动作　9. 修辞的
10. 特性　11. 讽刺　12. 寓言的

⛵ Vocabulary

folk	/fəʊk/	*adj.*	民俗的，传统的；流传民间的
humorous	/ˈhjuːmərəs/	*adj.*	幽默的，诙谐的
acquisition**	/ˌækwɪˈzɪʃn/	*n.*	获取；学得，习得
recount**	/rɪˈkaʊnt/	*v.*	叙述，说明
arduous**	/ˈɑːdʒuəs/	*adj.*	艰辛的，困难的
attainment*	/əˈteɪnmənt/	*n.*	获得；达到
righteous**	/ˈraɪtʃəs/	*adj.*	正直的，公正的
recite**	/rɪˈsaɪt/	*v.*	背诵，朗诵
cunning**	/ˈkʌnɪŋ/	*adj.*	狡猾的，诡诈的
likeable**	/ˈlaɪkəbl/	*adj.*	令人喜爱的，可爱的
regional	/ˈriːdʒənl/	*adj.*	地区的，区域的
perseverance**	/ˌpɜːsəˈvɪərəns/	*n.*	毅力，不屈不挠的精神
profound**	/prəˈfaʊnd/	*adj.*	（影响）深刻的，极大的

Exercises

A Decide whether the following statements are true (T) or false (F) according to the passage.

(　　) **1.** The author of *Journey to the West* is Wu Cheng'en, a novelist and poet of the Tang Dynasty.

(　　) **2.** The background of the novel is fabricated.

(　　) **3.** The Monkey King uses his magic powers to defeat all but the most powerful demons on the journey.

(　　) **4.** Sun Wukong can remove his headband by himself.

(　　) **5.** The novel is an entertaining adventure story.

B Fill in each blank with the proper form of the word given in the brackets.

1. His self-confidence and _____ (humor) conversations impressed us deeply.

2. He _____ (recount) to us his childhood adventures.

3. The _____ (attain) of his ambition was still a dream.

4. The _____ (regional) attracts tourists in their multitudes.

5. Memory can be _____ (profound) shaped by subsequent experiences.

C Complete the following sentences in English according to the Chinese.

1. 大蒜广泛应用于中国民间医药。
Garlic is widely used in Chinese _____ medicine.

2. 他们都义愤填膺。
They were filled with _____ indignation.

3. 背诵这篇文章不容易。
It is not easy to _____ this text.

4. 他从未停止努力，表现出了极大的毅力。
He has never stopped trying and showing great _____.

5. 那是一篇构思巧妙的侦探作品。

It was a _____ piece of detective work.

Text 2

Why Do We Love Music?

Today we have a question brought to us by Dreamworks Animations *Trolls*: Why do we love music so much?

Let's find out the answer on today's episode of Colossal Questions. Music has been around longer than humans have been recording history and almost all music lovers say they've loved it as long as they can remember.

Yet scientists still have no idea why we love music so much or what function it serves. But that certainly hasn't stopped the experts from trying to find out the answer.

Most researchers agree that music and dance are important forms of social communication that have connected communities for as long as humans have existed. After all, it's not just the trolls who've kept their friends and family close by singing and dancing together; cultures all across the globe have done the same throughout the century.

Experts have tried to find a music center in the brain. But no luck, it turns out that all different parts of brain are involved in the process of listening to and enjoying music.

A university study even took MRI scans of people while they listened to music and found that the limbic and paralymbic areas of the brain became extra active as blood flows to those regions. These are the same parts of the brain that kicks into gear anytime we do something that makes us feel really gleefully good. Everything from eating a really tasty meal to falling in love with your soul mate.

So while scientists continue to slowly unravel the mystery of why we love music, you can throw on your favorite song, turn it up and know for scientific certainty that music is awesome.

Exercise

Answer the following questions according to the passage.

1. What are the important forms of social communication?

_____

2. Do the scientists find out why we love music so much?

   _____

3. Which parts of brain are involved in the process of enjoying music?

   _____

4. Which areas of brain become extra active when people are doing something happy?

   _____

5. Do you love music? What kind of music do you like?

   _____

Part Three Writing

A Study the following sample about introducing a form of entertainment.

My favorite entertainment activity is the LARP (live action role playing) game, simply called script murder. It is an indoor activity that will help participants to build stronger relationships with friends. Players are each given a character with a complex backstory and costume, and are then thrown into an immersive environment to rummage around for clues and interact with other characters as they attempt to solve a crime. It is an effective way to help prevent dementia. To fully enjoy myself, I will call four or more friends to join me. We take part in this activity in my house almost one time a week. It can always bring excitement to me, which helps me to stay relaxed and forget my worries. I hope you can be one of us soon.

B Introduce your favorite entertainment activity with about 120 words.

_____

_____

_____

_____

_____

_____

_____

_____

_____

_____

C Complete the memo according to the Chinese information.

假定你是部门秘书 Alice Wang，以部门办公室的名义给全体员工发送一份内部通知。内容如下：

- 部门决定举行年度野餐；
- 举办时间为 5 月 15 日；
- 提供全部餐饮，还有奖品；
- 联系方式：秘书电话 555–2345；
- 5 月 10 日（星期一）前告知是否参加。

发送时间：2021 年 4 月 26 日

Memo

Date: (1)_____

To: All staff

From: Department office

Subject: (2)_____

    The annual department picnic (3)_____ on May 15th. (4)_____ are available. Prizes will be awarded to winners of the games. If you are interested, please (5)_____ the secretary at 555–2345 before Monday, May 10th.

Part Four ⛯ Speaking

A Read the following sentence patterns concerning entertainment.

Starter	Response
What's your best way to spend weekends?	I usually climb mountains to relax myself.
Are there any amusements that you can enjoy in your free time?	In my free time, I love to watch movies.
Shall we go to the cinema?	OK, let's go.
Do you know what's on tonight?	I heard that *The Speed* is on tonight.
May I ask you for a dance?	Sorry, I'm engaged. / Sure, it's my honor.
Are you a big fan of Rock & Roll?	Yes, I'm particularly into Rock music.
What's your favorite kind of movies?	My favorite movies are comedies.

B Complete the following dialogue with your own words.

Jessie: When I go to parties, I like to listen to party music.

Tim: (1)_____

Jessie: Loud music with fun lyrics that everyone can sing along with.

Tim: (2)_____

Jessie: Not really. Love songs are good when you are in the shower or by yourself.

Tim: (3)_____

Jessie: Some are OK, but they are usually too depressing.

Tim: (4)_____

Jessie: OK. Let's start with one of my favorites!

Tim: (5)_____

C Discuss with your partner the advantages and disadvantages of playing video games.

D Present your opinion on how teenagers can get rid of being addicted to playing video games.

Project   Introduce Your Favorite Means of Entertainment

Introduce your favorite means of entertainment in English within 2 minutes using PowerPoint slides.

UNIT **11**

Shopping

Warm-up

Choose the right option to complete the following dialogue.

> A. and the goods will be delivered to your home.
>
> B. Do you often shop online?
>
> C. 24 hours a day, seven days a week
>
> D. Maybe I should have a try.
>
> E. browse through many items and categories comfortably at home

Miss Jin: Your shoes look so cool. Where did you get them?

Mr. Wang: I bought them online.

Miss Jin: Really? (1)_____

Mr. Wang: Yes. Most of my clothes are bought from Taobao.

Miss Jin: I've never tried online shopping. Is it better than shopping at a physical store?

Mr. Wang: Yes, much better. You can log in a shopping APP, (2)_____, order the goods, pay by credit or debit card, (3)_____

Miss Jin: Sounds good, and I don't have to queue up at the cashier.

Mr. Wang: And you can still go "window shopping" just like in a real shopping mall.

Miss Jin: Well, are there any other advantages?

Mr. Wang: Yes, most of the shops are closed at 22:00 or even earlier, but the Internet operates (4)_____, and can be accessed anywhere.

Miss Jin: Are there many choices of online shopping?

Mr. Wang: Of course. You can buy almost anything you can think of.

Miss Jin: (5)_____

Part One 🗼 Listening

A Listen to the recording and choose the proper response.

1. A. Here it is.   B. I'm sorry to say so.
   C. Coffee, please.   D. See you next time.

2. A. Take it easy.   B. It's over there.
   C. This way, please.   D. I'm just looking.

3. A. Very good.   B. $200.
   C. That's nice.   D. It's far away.

4. A. Take your time.   B. It's over there.
   C. Never mind.   D. That's too large.

5. A. That's important.   B. No problem.
   C. Six months.   D. No, thanks.

B Listen to the dialogues and choose the best answer to each question.

1. A. Selecting a paint.   B. Asking directions.
   C. Trying on clothes.   D. Looking for something he lost.

2. A. Because he has not got enough money.
   B. Because he has been to other places.
   C. Because the motorcycles he has seen are not satisfactory.
   D. Because he will be away from home for weeks.

3. A. In a hotel.   B. In a stationery store.
   C. In a clothes store.   D. In a library.

4. A. Buying a car.   B. Selling a car.
   C. Buying a house.   D. Selling a house.

5. A. $4.00   B. $6.00
   C. $8.00   D. $12.00

C **Listen to the following dialogue and fill in the blanks with what you hear.**

(Rick and Sue are at home.)

Sue: Look. We're out of (1)_____. We need coffee for tomorrow morning. Can you go out and buy some?

Rick: Now? It's late. It's after 9:30 p.m. We can get it in the morning. I always wake up early. I can go shopping before (2)_____.

Sue: Tomorrow is Saturday. The store is always (3)_____ on Saturdays. I don't like to shop on the weekend. Anyway, we like to drink coffee in the morning.

Rick: But the (4)_____ is closed at night.

Sue: You're right. But the (5)_____ store is open. It's open 24/7.

Rick: My news program is on TV at 10:00 p.m. I don't have time before the news. It starts in 20 minutes.

Sue: You can go after the news.

(Rick is now at the convenience store. Sue calls him on his cell phone.)

Rick: Hello?

Sue: Hi. Are you at the convenience store now?

Rick: I'm still in the car. I'm in the (6)_____.

Sue: Can you go to the (7)_____ too and get some aspirin? I have a (8)_____.

Rick: Can I get the aspirin at the convenience store?

Sue: Yes, you can, but the aspirin is on sale this week at the pharmacy—two bottles for $7.00. It costs $7.00 for one bottle at the convenience store.

Rick: Which pharmacy?

Sue: The pharmacy near the convenience store. It's at the (9)_____. It's next to the (10)_____.

Rick: Is the pharmacy open late too?

Sue: Yes, it's open 24/7.

Part Two 🛕 Reading

Text 1

"Multi-channel" Shopping

Shoppers on Black Friday[1], the traditional start of the holiday shopping season in America, are very crazy. Some even start **queuing** outside stores before dawn[2] to be the first to get the heavily **discounted** goods. One year destructive[3] bargain-hunters[4] in the **suburbs** of New York City trampled[5] a Walmart employee to death. Despite the madness at many stores, however, the global[6] economic recession[7] appears to have accelerated[8] the pace at which shoppers are abandoning physical stores in favor of retailers[9] on the cyberspace[10] such as Amazon and eBay.

E-commerce **attracts** people in poor times as it enables them to compare prices across retailers quickly and easily. Buyers can sometimes avoid local sales taxes online, and shipping is often free. No wonder, then, that online shopping continues to grow even as the offline sort **declines**. The shift in spending to the Internet is good news for companies like P&G that lack retail shops of their own. But it is a big concern for **physical** retailers, whose prices are often higher than those of e-retailers, since they must bear the **extra** expense of running stores. The most obvious response to the trend for traditional retailers is to redouble their own efforts in the **virtual** space.

The concept of "multi-channel" shopping, where people can **purchase** the same items from the same retailer in several different ways online, via their mobile phones and in shops— is **gaining** ground, and retailers are trying to **motivate** users of one **channel** to try another. Growing online traffic[11] may actually increase sales in stores too. Retailers are also trying to make online shopping seem fun and exciting to act against the low economy. One common tactic[12] is to set up "pop-up" stores, which appear for a short time before disappearing again, to develop a sense of fashion and urgency[13].

Stores are also trying to lure[14] customers by offering services that are not **available** online. Best Buy, a consumer-electronics[15] retailer, has started selling music lessons along with its musical **instruments**. Lululemonathletica, which sells sports clothes, offers free yoga[16] classes. The idea is to bring people back to its shops regularly, increasing the likelihood that they will develop the **habit** of shopping there.

---

1. 黑色星期五（购物节） 2. 黎明，拂晓 3. 破坏性的;毁灭性的 4. 讨价还价者 5. 蹂躏,践踏 6. 全球的,全世界的 7. 经济衰退，经济不景气 8. 加速 9. 零售商 10. 网络空间 11. 通信量；流量 12. 方法，策略 13. 紧迫，急迫 14. 引诱，诱惑 15. 消费类电子产品 16. 瑜伽

⚓ Vocabulary

queue**	/kjuː/	*v.*	（人、车等）排队等候
discount	/dɪsˈkaʊnt/	*v.*	打折，减价出售
suburb	/ˈsʌbɜːb/	*n.*	郊区，城郊
attract	/əˈtrækt/	*v.*	吸引；使喜爱；引起……的好感（或爱慕）
decline*	/dɪˈklaɪn/	*v.*	减少，下降，衰落，衰退
physical	/ˈfɪzɪkl/	*adj.*	物质的，有形的；客观存在的，现实的
extra	/ˈekstrə/	*adj.*	额外的，分外的，外加的，附加的
virtual	/ˈvɜːtʃuəl/	*adj.*	模拟的，虚拟的；实质上的，事实上的
purchase	/ˈpɜːtʃəs/	*v.*	购买，采购
gain	/ɡeɪn/	*v.*	获得，赢得
motivate**	/ˈməʊtɪveɪt/	*v.*	激励，激发
channel	/ˈtʃænl/	*n.*	通道，渠道；频道；海峡
available	/əˈveɪləbl/	*adj.*	可获得的，可购得的，可找到的
instrument	/ˈɪnstrəmənt/	*n.*	器具，仪器；乐器
habit	/ˈhæbɪt/	*n.*	习惯；惯常行为

⚓ Exercises

A Decide whether the following statements are true (T) or false (F) according to the passage.

(   ) *1.* The writer mentioned Black Friday in the first paragraph to show how rude American shoppers are.

(   ) *2.* E-commerce benefits people by comparing prices across retailers quickly and easily, especially in poor times.

(   ) *3.* "Multi-channel" shopping means that people can purchase the same items from the same retailer in several different ways.

(   ) *4.* Sales in stores may be increased by the growing online traffic.

(   ) *5.* The writer's main purpose of writing the passage is to describe a form of business that is on the rise.

B Fill in each blanks with the proper form of the word given in the brackets.

1. They're offering a 10% _____ (discount) on all sofas this month.

2. What first _____ (attract) me to her was her sense of humor.

3. The company reported a small _____ (decline) in its profits.

4. The equipment can be _____ (purchase) from your local supplier.

5. The dress is _____ (available) in white or cream.

C Complete the following sentences in English according to the Chinese.

1. 一分耕耘一分收获，对吧?

No pain, no _____, right?

2. 那时东印度公司是孟加拉的实际统治者。

At that time the East India Company was the _____ ruler of Bengal.

3. 我们只得排一个小时的队买票。

We had to _____ up for an hour for the tickets.

4. 这个计划旨在促使员工更加卓有成效地工作。

The plan is designed to _____ employees to work more efficiently.

5. 这次会议将有很多额外工作。

The conference is going to have a lot of _____.

Text 2

Temple Fair

Temple fair, or *miaohui* in Chinese, was originally a gathering for sacrifice and pray to gods or Buddhas at temples. Going to temple fairs, also called "catching" or "touring" temple fairs, is an age-old tradition in China, especially in rural areas. The fair is usually set at or near temples. At fairs, operas are performed between worship activities. As temple fairs developed, more vendors joined in. They have become a combination of worship, entertainment and trade. In the past, entertainment and trade activities would not start until after the sacrificing ceremony.

Trade at a temple fair can be put into three categories:

First, indigenous products are available, both from the local area and from afar.

Second, food and toys are popular. The distinction of temple fairs from other markets or fairs is its entertaining spirit. Thus, the food and toy markets are especially lively. Restaurants, pubs and tea houses would build temporary tents with clothes or mats, or even set up business in the open air. Some vendors would go around at the fair seeking for potential customers. Toys are very popular at temple fairs: kites, masks, and bamboo or wood swords and spears, to name just a few.

Third, various folk shows are also popular, such as sword and spear playing, tricks and magic, monkey shows, puppet plays, rap operas, drum operas and circuses. At Penglaige and Yantai Yuhuangding temple fairs, not only are traditional trade and entertainment activities on display, but book fairs and other modern cultural events are held, combining traditional culture with modern life and bringing a new look to the temple fair.

⛵ Exercise

Answer the following questions according to the passage.

1. What did people originally do at a temple fair?

   _____

2. Where are temple fairs always held?

   _____

3. What kinds of goods can usually be found at a temple fair?

   _____

4. What do some vendors do at the temple fair?

   _____

5. Are temple fairs only held in Beijing? If not, where else do you know?

   _____

Part Three Writing

A Study the following sample about online shopping.

When it comes to online shopping, different people hold different ideas. Some people seem to enjoy the way of buying things online very much because they feel online shopping is so convenient. Some just don't believe that they can buy good quality commodities on the Internet. As far as I'm concerned, online shopping creates lots of benefits to people.

On the one hand, buying things online is a way of saving time. Compared with the traditional way of shopping, we do not need to go out to pick up our favorite goods from store to store. With just a click, we can have things in our shopping cart and just wait for the goods to be delivered to us. On the other hand, buying things online can save money. People buy commodities on the Internet not only because it saves time, but also because we can save lots of money. Online goods are usually cheaper than those displayed in shop windows because online shops do not need to pay the rent. So, people are more inclined to buying things from online stores.

In conclusion, online shopping is a convenient, time-saving and money-saving way of buying things. We can benefit a lot from it. That's why it has developed faster and faster in recent years.

B Study the following chart and write down your attitude towards online grocery shopping.

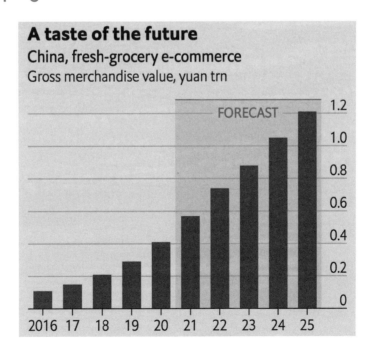

A taste of the future
China, fresh-grocery e-commerce
Gross merchandise value, yuan trn

_____

_____

_____

_____

_____

_____

_____

_____

_____

_____

C **Complete the complaint letter according to the Chinese information.**

假设你是马丹丹，本周二在一家商店买了一部手机，第二天便发现手机无法接听和拨打电话，有时还会自动关机，并因此而错过一位客户的重要电话。现打算给这家商店写一封投诉信，要求退款。

写信日期：2021 年 4 月 28 日

(1)_____

Dear Sir or Madam,

    I am (2)_____. I feel bad to trouble you, but I am afraid that I have to make a complaint about (3)_____ I bought this Tuesday.

The reason for my dissatisfaction is that the mobile phone was unable to (4)_____ the next day, and sometimes shut down automatically. Therefore, I missed an important call from a customer.

I appreciate it very much if you could give me (5) _____, and I would like to have this matter settled as soon as possible.

Thank you for your consideration and I will be looking forward to your reply.

Yours sincerely,

Ma Dandan

Part Four Speaking

A Read the following sentence patterns concerning shopping.

Shop Assistant	Customer
What can I do for you? May I help you?	Can you show me that pair of shoes? Can I have a look at this shirt? I'm looking for a shirt for my husband. I'd like to have a look at this shirt.
Any particular color? What size do you want?	I prefer black. Do you have this in size 10? Have you got any bigger sizes?
The price is reasonable. It is really a bargain. Lucky you, you can get it at an attractive price. You can enjoy a 10% discount right now!	How much are they? What's the price for it? Do you have anything cheaper? Are these trousers on sale? That's too much.
We provide our customers with a long-term after-sale service.	I'll take it.

B Complete the following dialogue with your own words.

Shop assistant:　Good morning, sir! (1)_____

Customer:　(2)_____ that smart phone please?

Shop assistant:　Yes, of course. This is a really good one actually.

Customer:　(3)_____

Shop assistant:　This one is 1,500 yuan.

Customer:　It looks pretty good. (4)_____

Shop assistant:　Would you like anything else?

Customer:　(5)_____

C Introduce something you have just bought in English.

D Discuss with your partner the different attitudes towards bargaining between people at home and abroad.

Project　Make up a Shopping Dialogue

Make up a shopping dialogue with more than 10 sentences and act it out with your partner.

UNIT 12

Job

Warm-up

Choose the right option to complete the following dialogue.

> A. I'll inform you of the result.
>
> B. But I need a part-time job.
>
> C. I can communicate well with customers.
>
> D. Why do you apply for a job in our company?
>
> E. Nice to meet you.

Paul: Hello, I'm Paul, the owner of the company. (1)_____ Please sit down.

Smith: Thank you, Mr. Paul. Nice to meet you, too.

Paul: Welcome to our company.

Smith: Thank you for arranging this interview for me.

Paul: My pleasure. (2)_____

Smith: Your company is suitable for me.

Paul: What is your current job?

Smith: I'm a seller. The job is fantastic. (3)_____ I want to have more time to take care of my sons.

Paul: What skills do you have that might be beneficial for working here at my company?

Smith: (4)_____ I'm really good at working with others.

Paul: That's nice. Thank you for coming today. (5)_____ Take care.

Smith: Thank you so much.

Part One ⚓ Listening

A Listen to the recording and choose the proper response.

1. A. Sorry, I don't know.　　　　B. It's over there.
   C. I'm a student.　　　　　　　D. In a local hospital.

2. A. That's OK.　　　　　　　　B. Boring.
   C. Thank you.　　　　　　　　D. No problem.

3. A. An engineer.　　　　　　　B. Very much.
   C. In the office.　　　　　　　D. So do I.

4. A. No problem.　　　　　　　B. Yes, I have.
   C. No, I didn't.　　　　　　　D. Yes, I will.

5. A. That's good.　　　　　　　B. No, I didn't.
   C. Yes, I do.　　　　　　　　D. Not bad.

B Listen to the dialogues and choose the best answer to each question.

1. A. 71, Yan'an Road (West), Suite 6, Building No. 1, Shanghai.
   B. 6, Yan'an Road (West), Suite 71, Building No. 1, Shanghai.
   C. 6, Yan'an Road (West), Suite 1, Building No. 71, Shanghai.
   D. 1, Yan'an Road (West), Suite 6, Building No. 71, Shanghai.

2. A. He majors in practical mathematics.
   B. His minor is physics.
   C. His major is physics.
   D. His minor is mechanics.

3. A. She didn't work hard at them.
   B. She was very diligent in college.
   C. Her scores of major subjects dropped.
   D. She didn't find them very interesting.

4. A. A post in an advertisement company.
   B. A teaching post.
   C. A cleaning job.
   D. A job where English is used.

5. A. The candidate can speak English, but not fluently.

   B. The job requires a good knowledge of written English.

   C. The candidate does not like the job at all.

   D. The candidate can speak English fluently.

C Listen to the following dialogue and fill in the blanks with what you hear.

Interviewer: Hello, thank you for coming today.

Interviewee: Thanks. Nice to meet you.

Interviewer: Nice to meet you, too. Could you please (1)_____ yourself briefly?

Interviewee: OK. I'm Chen Yong. I graduated from (2)_____. I'm coming for your advertisement for a chemical process draftsman.

Interviewer: Well, for this job, we need people to work hard. Do you think you're suitable for this kind of job?

Interviewee: Yes, I'm (3)_____, (4)_____ and (5)_____ in any project I undertake.

Interviewer: Have you got any working experience?

Interviewee: I worked as the (6)_____ of a draftsman in a factory during the summer vacation this year.

Interviewer: Why do you (7)_____ the job in our company?

Interviewee: Well, I'd like to work in a large company like yours that provides many (8)_____ for growth.

Interviewer: Would you like to talk about your (9)_____ requirements?

Interviewee: I believe that your company will deal with this issue friendly and reasonably.

Interviewer: Mr. Chen, it seems that you have the qualifications. Please fill in the (10)_____. You'll be hearing from us in two weeks.

Interviewee: Thank you for giving me the chance.

Part Two 🏠 Reading

Text 1

Job

Most people in modern society spend more than eight hours a day working. Some are successful in their jobs, but many more are under stress. Workers are **classified** into two groups: self-employed and **employees**. An interesting fact is that the self-employed **envy** the employees, and vice versa[1]. The reason? People tend to exaggerate[2] the others' benefits they don't have.

Businessmen seem to have greater **satisfaction** from their jobs than **ordinary** workers do. They have the power to decide things by themselves. That's why ordinary workers are envious of them. But businessmen must take **responsibility** for their decisions, and if something goes wrong, they could go bankrupt[3].

Every employee has a certain job responsibility, but if he does what he is expected to, he is usually exempt[4] from bad consequences[5]. He has a stable[6] position. On the other hand, a competent[7] worker may enjoy many promotions and **raises**, but still be at the **mercy** of the manipulations[8] of **corporate executives**.

Who is happier is not the question. The important thing is that people must decide which **category** they should belong to by **evaluating** themselves honestly.

People have different priorities in getting jobs. Some put their emphasis on making more money, others want job security[9], promotion opportunities, and work they are comfortable with. As for me, I want my own business. After I quit my first job I never thought about working for anyone again. When I work for someone else and can't sell my ideas to the boss, that **disappoints** me. And often employees become the scapegoats[10] for marketing failures. I love to work alone with my ideas and plans, knowing whether my business succeeds or not is up to me.

I really want to have my own business, as most employees do. But a boss must have many special characteristics. First of all, he must have creative ideas and know when, where, and how to apply them. Moreover, he must have the nerve to go ahead with his plans against difficult markets. He also must cultivate[11] customers, because success largely depends upon human relationships. If he has solid relationships with his business partners, he may be able to make up for temporary[12] **financial** straits[13].

---

1. 反之亦然　2. 夸张，夸大　3. 破产的　4. 被免除的　5. 后果　6. 稳定的　7. 有能力胜任的　8. 操作；处理　9. 安全　10. 替罪羊　11. 培育　12. 临时的　13. 困境

Vocabulary

classify**	/'klæsɪfaɪ/	v.	分类，分等
employee*	/ɪm'plɔɪiː/	n.	雇员，雇工
envy**	/'envi/	n.	羡慕；嫉妒
satisfaction**	/ˌsætɪs'fækʃn/	n.	满足，满意
ordinary	/'ɔːdnri/	adj.	普通的，平常的
responsibility	/rɪˌspɒnsə'bɪləti/	n.	职责，责任
raise	/reɪz/	n.	加薪
mercy**	/'mɜːsi/	n.	仁慈，宽容
corporate**	/'kɔːpərət/	adj.	公司的；法人的
executive**	/ɪg'zekjətɪv/	n.	主管；执行官
category*	/'kætəgəri/	n.	种类，类别
evaluate**	/ɪ'væljueɪt/	v.	评价；估价
disappoint	/ˌdɪsə'pɔɪnt/	v.	使失望
financial**	/faɪ'nænʃl/	adj.	财政的；金融的

Exercises

A Decide whether the following statements are true (T) or false (F) according to the passage.

(   ) 1. Most people in modern society work less than eight hours a day.

(   ) 2. A competent worker may enjoy many promotions and raises, and can escape the manipulations of corporate executives.

(   ) 3. It is important that people decide which category they should belong to by honestly evaluating themselves.

(   ) 4. Employees are often the scapegoats for marketing failures.

(   ) 5. Success largely depends on interpersonal relationships.

B Fill in each blank with the proper form of the word given in the brackets.

1. If the item is not _____ (satisfy), you will get your money back.

2. He still felt _____ (response) for her death.

3. He was soon _____ (promote) to the rank of captain.

4. They believed, correctly, that IQ tests are a valid method of _____ (evaluate) children for special education classes.

5. The museum is in a _____ (financial) precarious position.

C **Complete the following sentences in English according to the Chinese.**

1. 她心中充满嫉妒和憎恨。

She was devoured by _____ and hatred.

2. 企业破产的数量 8 月份增加了。

The number of _____ bankruptcies climbed in August.

3. 评委们无法判定它属于哪一类。

The judges could not decide which _____ it belonged to.

4. 无论我们如何对服务进行分类，这都是真的。

This is true regardless of how we _____ the service.

5. 我把自己归类为一名普通的劳动者。

I class myself as an _____ working person.

Text **2**

Etiquette to Pay Attention to in a Job Interview

Etiquette 1: Image Problem

After arriving at the interview place, pay attention to the interview etiquette and don't look around. It is better to mute or turn off the phone before the interview. Enter the interview unit and wait patiently in the waiting area as directed by the front desk clerk. After arriving at the office, knock on the door and ask the interviewer first.

Etiquette 2: Pay Attention to Time Concept

The concept of time is very important. It is best to arrive at the interview place about ten minutes in advance during the interview. Interviewers can be late. You should not mind the late interviewers, otherwise the recruiters' first impression on you will be lowered, even leading to a loss in the whole set.

Etiquette 3: Details Decide Success or Failure

During the interview, when your name is called, you should knock at the door before entering. Don't knock too hard and enter the room after hearing people inside say, "Please come in". Open the door and gently close it with your hand. Sit in a sitting position. If you have a chair, sit about two-thirds of the chair; the upper body should be straight; keep a relaxed posture; don't cross your arms in front of your chest. You can't put your hand on the back of the seat next to you, or do some little tricks.

Etiquette 4: Self-introduction

Self-introduction can reflect a person's wisdom and moral quality, short and rich in connotation. Minute description will leave a deep impression on the interviewer. Don't be nervous when you speak, or you may end up with incoherent words.

 **Exercise**

Answer the following questions according to the passage.

1. How many kinds of manners about interview are mentioned in the passage?

    _____

2. How long should you arrive at the interview site in advance?

    _____

3. What should you do when the interviewer is late?

    _____

4. What should you do before you walk through the door at the interview?

    _____

5. What can self-introduction reflect?

    _____

Part Three  Writing

A Study the following sample application letter.

Dear Sir,

Your advertisement for a worker in foreign trade business interested me, because the position you described sounds pretty like the job I'm seeking for.

I've worked in a foreign trade business in Shenzhen for two years. On the one hand, I track the goods which are exported abroad. On the other hand, I develop foreign customers. And also I'm the assistant of a vice president. I am responsible for many businesses in the company, such as arranging the meetings, translating the English documents and so on. I'm able to communicate with foreign customers fluently. My English is pretty good.

I'm looking forward to having a chance to attend your interview.

Enclosed is my resume. If you want any additional information, please contact me freely.

Thanks and best regards.

Yours faithfully,

Wang Tingting

B Write an application letter for a job of English teacher, which is advertised on a newspaper.

_____

_____

_____

_____

_____

_____

C Complete the resume according to the Chinese information.

假设你叫王军，男，1992 年 6 月 26 日出生，未婚，家住南京市中山路 55 号。2014 年 6 月从苏州职业大学计算机系毕业。曾在一家软件公司兼职三年。具有较强的交际能力，英语口语流利。愿意接受新的挑战，责任意识强。欲求计算机程序员职位。

Resume

Name: Wang Jun

Address: (1)_____

Date of birth: (2)_____

Gender: (3)_____

Marital status: unmarried

Job objective: (4)_____

Education:

(5)_____

_____

Work experience:

(6)_____

Strong points:

(7)_____

_____

Part Four 🗼 Speaking

A Read the following sentence patterns concerning jobs.

Starter	Response
What sort of job do you have in mind?	I am interested in the position of...
Do you have any jobs for a part-timer?	Yes, we have...
What qualifications and experience do you have?	I am almost straight A from school.
Do you think a cleaning job could appeal to you?	I'm afraid not.
How can I get an on-campus job?	You may apply to the Student Employment Service.
Can you tell me what your greatest advantage is?	I can...

B Complete the following dialogue with your own words.

Li Ming: How many forms of resumes do you know? What are they?

Peter Brown: (1)_____

Li Ming: What elements does Basic Resume typically include?

Peter Brown: (2)_____

Li Ming: What is the order of experience and education in Experience-oriented Resume?

Peter Brown: (3)_____

Li Ming: What is similar in Experience-oriented Resume and Functional Resume?

Peter Brown: (4)_____

Li Ming: What is the fundamental difference between Experience-oriented Resume and Functional Resume?

Peter Brown: (5)_____

C Interview someone about his/her part-time job in English, such as your best friend or the graduate of your school.

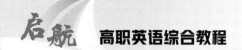

D Discuss with your partner how to answer the questions an interviewer may propose. For example, what is your greatest strength/weakness? Can you introduce yourself briefly? Why do you think we should hire you? What is your salary expectation? Why do you want this job? How do you handle stress? What are your goals for the future?

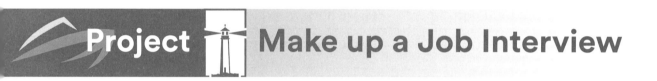

Project 🗼 Make up a Job Interview

Make up an English job interview using your resume and act it out with your partner.

Glossary

A

achieve	/ə'tʃi:v/	v.	实现；获得	Uint 3
acquisition**	/ˌækwɪ'zɪʃn/	n.	获取；学得，习得	Uint 10
adapt	/ə'dæpt/	v.	（使）适应	Uint 3
adventurous**	/əd'ventʃərəs/	adj.	有冒险精神的	Uint 9
affect*	/ə'fekt/	v.	影响	Uint 2
analysis**	/ə'næləsɪs/	n.	（对事物的）分析；分析结果	Uint 1
annual	/'ænjuəl/	adj.	每年的，年度的	Uint 7
apply	/ə'plaɪ/	v.	申请，请求	Uint 1
approach	/ə'prəʊtʃ/	v./n.	临近，接近；方式，方法	Uint 8
arduous**	/'ɑ:dʒuəs/	adj.	艰辛的，困难的	Uint 10
aspect	/'æspekt/	n.	方面	Uint 5
assignment**	/ə'saɪnmənt/	n.	作业；任务	Uint 8
athlete	/'æθli:t/	n.	运动员	Uint 6
atmosphere*	/'ætməsfɪə(r)/	n.	气氛；大气	Uint 7
attacker**	/ə'tækə(r)/	n.	攻击者，进攻者	Uint 6
attainment*	/ə'teɪnmənt/	n.	获得；达到	Uint 10
attempt	/ə'tempt/	n.	尝试，试图，企图	Uint 2
attract	/ə'trækt/	v.	吸引；使喜爱；引起……的好感（或爱慕）	Uint 11
available	/ə'veɪləbl/	adj.	可获得的，可购得的，可找到的	Uint 11
avoid	/ə'vɔɪd/	v.	避免	Uint 8

B

bacon	/'beɪkən/	n.	熏猪肉；培根肉	Uint 5
basic	/'beɪsɪk/	adj.	基本的，基础的	Uint 6
biologically**	/ˌbaɪə'lɒdʒɪkli/	adv.	生物学上，生物学地	Uint 6
biscuit	/'bɪskɪt/	n.	饼干	Uint 5
blog**	/blɒg/	n.	博客	Uint 9
butter	/'bʌtə(r)/	n.	黄油	Uint 5

C

calendar	/ˈkælɪndə(r)/	n.	日历	Uint 7
category*	/ˈkætəgəri/	n.	种类，类别	Uint 12
celebrate	/ˈselɪbreɪt/	v.	庆祝；过节；祝贺	Uint 7
challenge	/ˈtʃælɪndʒ/	n.	挑战	Uint 3
channel	/ˈtʃænl/	n.	通道，渠道；频道；海峡	Uint 11
classify**	/ˈklæsɪfaɪ/	v.	分类，分等	Uint 12
comfort*	/ˈkʌmfət/	n.	舒适，安慰	Uint 5
commit**	/kəˈmɪt/	v.	做出（错事）；犯罪	Uint 2
continuous**	/kənˈtɪnjuəs/	adj.	连续的，持续的	Uint 7
convenient	/kənˈviːniənt/	adj.	方便的	Uint 8
corporate**	/ˈkɔːpərət/	adj.	公司的；法人的	Uint 12
crazy	/ˈkreɪzi/	adj.	疯狂的，狂热的	Uint 6
creative	/kriˈeɪtɪv/	adj.	创造性的	Uint 8
critical*	/ˈkrɪtɪkl/	adj.	极重要的；关键的	Uint 2
cunning**	/ˈkʌnɪŋ/	adj.	狡猾的，诡诈的	Uint 10

D

dairy	/ˈdeəri/	n.	乳制品	Uint 4
decline*	/dɪˈklaɪn/	v.	减少，下降，衰落，衰退	Uint 11
delay	/dɪˈleɪ/	v.	耽搁，延误	Uint 3
deliver	/dɪˈlɪvə(r)/	v.	发表；传递，投递；交付	Uint 7
determine	/dɪˈtɜːmɪn/	v.	判定；确定；作出决定，下决心	Uint 8
digitally	/ˈdɪdʒɪtli/	adv.	数码地；数字地	Uint 7
disappoint	/ˌdɪsəˈpɔɪnt/	v.	使失望	Uint 12
discount	/dɪsˈkaʊnt/	v.	打折，减价出售	Uint 11
distraction**	/dɪˈstrækʃn/	n.	分心的事物；干扰	Uint 3
domesticate**	/dəˈmestɪkeɪt/	v.	驯化	Uint 6
donation	/dəʊˈneɪʃn/	n.	捐款	Uint 8

E

effect	/ɪˈfekt/	n.	影响；效果	Uint 2
employee*	/ɪmˈplɔɪiː/	n.	雇员，雇工	Uint 12
envy**	/ˈenvi/	n.	羡慕；嫉妒	Uint 12

essentially	/ɪˈsenʃəli/	adv.	本质上；本来	Uint 6
establish	/ɪˈstæblɪʃ/	v.	建立，创立，设立	Uint 1
evaluate**	/ɪˈvæljueɪt/	v.	评价；估价	Uint 12
executive**	/ɪɡˈzekjətɪv/	n.	主管；执行官	Uint 12
experience	/ɪkˈspɪəriəns/	n.	（一次）经历，体验	Uint 9
explore	/ɪkˈsplɔː(r)/	v.	探索，探险	Uint 9
expose*	/ekˈspəʊz/	v.	显示；揭露	Uint 8
extra	/ˈekstrə/	adj.	额外的，分外的，外加的，附加的	Uint 11
extraordinary**	/ɪkˈstrɔːdnri/	adj.	非凡的；特别的	Uint 1

F

factor	/ˈfæktə(r)/	n.	因素，要素	Uint 2
feature	/ˈfiːtʃə(r)/	v.	由……主演	Uint 9
fiber**	/ˈfaɪbə(r)/	n.	（食物中的）纤维素	Uint 4
financial**	/faɪˈnænʃl/	adj.	财政的；金融的	Uint 12
folk	/fəʊk/	adj.	民俗的，传统的；流传民间的	Uint 10
foreigner	/ˈfɒrənə(r)/	n.	外国人	Uint 5
foundation**	/faʊnˈdeɪʃn/	n.	基础；基金会	Uint 1
frequently	/ˈfriːkwəntli/	adv.	频繁地	Uint 5

G

gain	/ɡeɪn/	v.	获得，赢得	Uint 11
generous	/ˈdʒenərəs/	adj.	慷慨的，大方的；有雅量的	Uint 2
grain**	/ɡreɪn/	n.	谷物，谷粒	Uint 4
grocery	/ˈɡrəʊsəri/	n.	食品杂货店	Uint 1
guideline	/ˈɡaɪdlaɪn/	n.	指导方针；准则	Uint 4

H

| habit | /ˈhæbɪt/ | n. | 习惯；惯常行为 | Uint 11 |
| humorous | /ˈhjuːmərəs/ | adj. | 幽默的，诙谐的 | Uint 10 |

I

| identify* | /aɪˈdentɪfaɪ/ | v. | 辨别；确定 | Uint 8 |
| ignore | /ɪɡˈnɔː(r)/ | v. | 忽视；对……不予理会 | Uint 9 |

impact	/'ɪmpækt/	v.	影响	Uint 2
indicate	/'ɪndɪkeɪt/	v.	表明；显示	Uint 4
informal*	/ɪn'fɔːml/	adj.	不正式的	Uint 5
instrument	/'ɪnstrəmənt/	n.	器具，仪器；乐器	Uint 11
intelligence	/ɪn'telɪdʒəns/	n.	智力，智慧	Uint 6
interruption*	/ˌɪntə'rʌpʃn/	n.	干扰，中断	Uint 3
inventive**	/ɪn'ventɪv/	adj.	有创造力的	Uint 8
investment*	/ɪn'vestmənt/	n.	投资	Uint 1
involve*	/ɪn'vɒlv/	v.	包含，涉及	Uint 6

J

jam	/dʒæm/	n.	果酱	Uint 5

K

keen*	/kiːn/	adj.	（对……）着迷的，渴望的；热心的	Uint 1

L

landmark**	/'lændmɑːk/	n.	地标	Uint 9
likeable**	/'laɪkəbl/	adj.	令人喜爱的，可爱的	Uint 10
link	/lɪŋk/	v.	连接；联合	Uint 2
local	/'ləʊkl/	adj.	当地的，本地的	Uint 9
lunar	/'luːnə(r)/	adj.	阴历的；月球的	Uint 7

M

maintain	/meɪn'teɪn/	v.	维持，保持	Uint 3
management	/'mænɪdʒmənt/	n.	管理	Uint 3
measure	/'meʒə(r)/	v.	测量	Uint 8
mercy**	/'mɜːsi/	n.	仁慈，宽容	Uint 12
mineral*	/'mɪnərəl/	n.	矿物质；矿物	Uint 4
motivate**	/'məʊtɪveɪt/	v.	激励，激发	Uint 11

N

necessity**	/nə'sesəti/	n.	必要，需要	Uint 6
nutrient**	/'njuːtriənt/	n.	营养素，营养物	Uint 4

O

ordinary	/'ɔ:dnri/	*adj.*	普通的，平常的	Uint 12
origin**	/'ɒrɪdʒɪn/	*n.*	起源	Uint 5
outcome*	/'aʊtkʌm/	*n.*	结果；效果	Uint 1
overall	/ˌəʊvə'rɔ:l/	*adj.*	整体的；全部的	Uint 3

P

payment**	/'peɪmənt/	*n.*	支付，付款；报酬	Uint 7
peak*	/pi:k/	*n.*	最高点；峰值	Uint 2
philosophy**	/fə'lɒsəfi/	*n.*	哲学	Uint 1
physical	/'fɪzɪkl/	*adj.*	物质的，有形的；客观存在的，现实的	Uint 11
perseverance**	/ˌpɜ:sə'vɪərəns/	*n.*	毅力，不屈不挠的精神	Uint 10
popularization**	/ˌpɒpjələraɪ'zeɪʃn/	*n.*	普及，大众化	Uint 7
predictable**	/prɪ'dɪktəbl/	*adj.*	可预见的，可预料的	Uint 9
professional**	/prə'feʃnl/	*adj.*	职业的，专业的	Uint 6
profound**	/prə'faʊnd/	*adj.*	（影响）深刻的，极大的	Uint 10
promote	/prə'məʊt/	*v.*	促进；推动	Uint 4
purchase	/'pɜ:tʃəs/	*v.*	购买，采购	Uint 11

Q

| queue** | /kju:/ | *v.* | （人、车等）排队等候 | Uint 11 |

R

raise	/reɪz/	*n.*	加薪	Uint 12
recite**	/rɪ'saɪt/	*v.*	背诵，朗诵	Uint 10
recommend	/ˌrekə'mend/	*v.*	推荐，举荐；介绍	Uint 4
recommendation	/ˌrekəmen'deɪʃn/	*n.*	推荐；介绍	Uint 9
recount**	/rɪ'kaʊnt/	*v.*	叙述，说明	Uint 10
regard	/rɪ'gɑ:d/	*v.*	把……看作	Uint 5
regional	/'ri:dʒənl/	*adj.*	地区的，区域的	Uint 10
register*	/'redʒɪstə(r)/	*v.*	登记；注册	Uint 10
regularly	/'regjələli/	*adv.*	有规律地	Uint 5
reservation**	/ˌrezə'veɪʃn/	*n.*	预订，保留	Uint 8
reserve**	/rɪ'zɜ:v/	*v.*	预留	Uint 3

respond	/rɪˈspɒnd/	v.	回应；对……作出反应	Uint 2
responsibility	/rɪˌspɒnsəˈbɪləti/	n.	职责，责任	Uint 12
reunion	/ˌriːˈjuːniən/	n.	团聚，重逢，聚会	Uint 7
review	/rɪˈvjuː/	v.	回顾；复习	Uint 3
righteous**	/ˈraɪtʃəs/	adj.	正直的，公正的	Uint 10
ripe**	/raɪp/	adj.	成熟的	Uint 1
risk	/rɪsk/	n.	危险，风险	Uint 4
rural*	/ˈrʊərəl/	adj.	乡村的，农村的	Uint 1
rush	/rʌʃ/	v.	迅速移动；急着（做）	Uint 9

S

satisfaction**	/ˌsætɪsˈfækʃn/	n.	满足，满意	Uint 12
sausage	/ˈsɒsɪdʒ/	n.	香肠	Uint 5
schedule	/ˈʃedjuːl/	n.	计划表；时间表	Uint 3
sensible*	/ˈsensəbl/	adj.	合理的；明智的	Uint 3
seriously	/ˈsɪəriəsli/	adv.	认真地；严肃地	Uint 8
sight	/saɪt/	n.	名胜，风景	Uint 9
similar	/ˈsɪmələ(r)/	adj.	相似的	Uint 7
snack	/snæk/	n.	零食；小吃；快餐	Uint 4
source	/sɔːs/	n.	来源，出处	Uint 4
specific	/spəˈsɪfɪk/	adj.	特定的，特殊的	Uint 8
standard	/ˈstændəd/	n.	标准，水平；规格，规范	Uint 1
starvation**	/stɑːˈveɪʃn/	n.	饥饿，挨饿	Uint 6
stock	/stɒk/	n.	股票；股份	Uint 1
subject	/ˈsʌbdʒɪkt/	n.	接受试验者，实验对象	Uint 2
suburb	/ˈsʌbɜːb/	n.	郊区，城郊	Uint 11
survival	/səˈvaɪvl/	n.	幸存，生存	Uint 6
symbolize**	/ˈsɪmbəlaɪz/	v.	象征；用符号表现	Uint 7

T

totally	/ˈtəʊtəli/	adv.	完全地	Uint 8
track	/træk/	v.	追踪，跟踪	Uint 3
traditional	/trəˈdɪʃənl/	adj.	传统的	Uint 5
transfer	/trænsˈfɜː(r)/	v.	转学；调动；转移	Uint 1

| transformation** | /ˌtrænsfəˈmeɪʃn/ | *n.* | 变化，转变 | Uint 6 |
| trend* | /trend/ | *v.* | 有……的趋势，趋向 | Uint 9 |

U

| upper | /ˈʌpə(r)/ | *adj.* | 上等的；上面的 | Uint 5 |

V

variety**	/vəˈraɪəti/	*n.*	多样；种类	Uint 7
virtual	/ˈvɜːtʃuəl/	*adj.*	模拟的，虚拟的；实质上的，事实上的	Uint 11
vital**	/ˈvaɪtl/	*adj.*	极其重要的；必不可少的	Uint 6
vitamin*	/ˈvɪtəmɪn/	*n.*	维生素	Uint 4

W

| wander* | /ˈwɒndə(r)/ | *v.* | （指人或动物）离开原处或正道 | Uint 9 |

Y

| yoghurt* | /ˈjɒgət/ | *n.* | 酸奶 | Uint 4 |